COMPELLING CONVERSATIONS: VIETNAM

Speaking Exercises for Vietnamese Learners of English

Written by:
Teresa X. Nguyen and Eric H. Roth

Edited by:
Toni Aberson

Compelling Conversations – Vietnam:
Speaking Exercises for Vietnamese Learners of English 2nd Edition
978-0-9904988-3-4
paperback black & white - 8.5 x 11

978-0-9904988-7-2
paperback color - 8 x10 paperback

978-0-9904988-2-7
ebook

Library of Congress Control Number:
2016950549

Publisher's Cataloging-in-Publication
(Provided by Quality Books, Inc.)
Nguyen, Teresa X., author.
Compelling conversations--Vietnam:
speaking exercises for Vietnamese Learners of English/Teresa X. Nguyen and Eric H. Roth;
edited by Toni Aberson. – 2nd edition.
pages cm.
Includes bibliographical references.
LCCN 2016950549
ISBN 978-0-9904988-3-4 (paperback) – 8.5 x 11 black and white
ISBN 978-0-9904988-7-2 (paperback) – 8 x 10 color
ISBN 978-0-9904988-2-7 (e-book)

---

1. English language--Textbooks for foreign speakers--Vietnamese.
2. English language--Conversation and phrase books--Vietnamese.
3. Quotations, English.
4. Textbooks.
5. Phrase books.
6. Quotations.
I. Roth, Eric H. (Eric Hermann), 1961- author.
II. Aberson, Toni, editor.
III. Expanded version of (work): Roth, Eric H. (Eric Hermann), 1961- Compelling conversations Volume 1.
IV. Title.
PE1130.V5N475 2017 428.3'495922
QBI16-900067

Chimayo Press

3766 Redwood Avenue
Los Angeles, California
90066-3506
United States of America
+1.310.390.0131
www.ChimayoPress.com
www.CompellingConversations.com

Dedicated to

Dani Herbert Joseph Roth
(1937—1997)
A global citizen, he could talk with almost anyone, in six different languages, and share a laugh.

"Kindness is the language
which the deaf can hear and the blind can see."
—Mark Twain (1835-1910),
American author

"One cannot always be a hero,
but one can always be human."
—Johann Wolfgang von Goethe ((1749-1832),
German playwright, novelist, and scientist

Eric H. Roth

Dedicated to my parents, whose struggles inspired me to be part of such a creative piece. And dedicated to my significant other, who supported me being me.

Teresa X. Nguyen

PREFACE

How do we help our Vietnamese students develop their conversation and discussion skills in English? This fluency-focused ESL book provides our long answer to that simple question.

Text Organization

Each chapter follows a similar format designed to learn and practice meaningful conversations in a real context:

1. **Getting Started:** This short activity introduces the chapter theme.
2. **Sharing Experiences:** A set of 15 questions sparks conversations for a pair to practice speaking skills.
3. **Word List:** This list provides 12 vocabulary words and Vietnamese phonemes for study and use in each chapter.
4. **Expanding Vocabulary:** The 12 vocabulary words are defined with sample sentences, concluding with students practicing by writing questions with the new words.
5. **Asking Questions with New Vocabulary Words:** Students write four questions using the new vocabulary words. Instructors provide feedback.
6. **Paraphrasing Proverbs:** A small set of Vietnamese and international proverbs to build paraphrasing skills and convey ideas in different ways.
7. **Building Words:** Each chapter introduces a prefix or suffix. Students complete charts to practice identifying the meanings of other words that incorporate the same feature. Students learn to systematically study English words and expand their working academic vocabulary.
8. **Discussing Quotations:** Students in small groups read and evaluate famous quotations by important cultural figures. Then students say whether they agree or disagree, explain their opinions, and choose a favorite quote.
9. **The Conversation Continues:** This second set of more difficult conversation questions takes a deeper look at the topic, often using new vocabulary words. We suggest students work with a different partner to build fluency.
10. **Pronunciation Corner:** This exercise helps students improve the accuracy of pronunciation and focuses on common pronunciation problems for Vietnamese learners of English.
11. **Culture Corner:** A short explanation of American cultural tips to help students better understand and feel more comfortable in the United States.

Appendices

The text also includes a few appendices so students can continue to develop their speaking skills in English and become more autotelic (self-driven) learners.

We hope that this fluency-focused ESL textbook meets the needs of your students.

To the Student

Speaking English clearly and creating memorable conversations in English can open many new doors for you in the United States and around the world.

Do you want to make new international friends? Do you want to talk about movies, restaurants, and memories with native English speakers? Or perhaps you want a better job? Or do you plan to succeed in an American college and need to participate more in class discussions? Have you considered traveling and using English as an international language? Have you wondered about living in Australia, England, or the United States?

This American English conversation textbook for Vietnamese English language learners will help you become more fluent in English. As you become more confident speaking English and sharing your experiences in English, you may find yourself dreaming in English too.

These activities can help you:

- **Ask** clear, simple questions in English
- **Listen** to each other in English
- **Respond** to questions in English
- **Understand** other English speakers better
- **Become** more comfortable speaking English
- **Use** common conversation starters in English
- **Learn** how to continue conversations on many topics
- **Discover** and **use** new English vocabulary words
- **Memorize** some American sayings
- **Recall** some Vietnamese and international proverbs in English
- **Discuss** ideas by studying classical and modern quotations in English
- **Express** your opinions and support your statements in English
- **Find** and **share** Internet resources about modern life in English
- **Speak** English with greater confidence in the United States and abroad
- **Learn** more about your classmates and yourself in English

You may have heard the phrase "practice makes perfect." We prefer the more practical observation that "Practice makes progress." Our goal is for you to make significant, meaningful, and verifiable progress in every chapter.

You will learn by doing and creating real, meaningful conversations in English. Let's begin!

CONTENTS

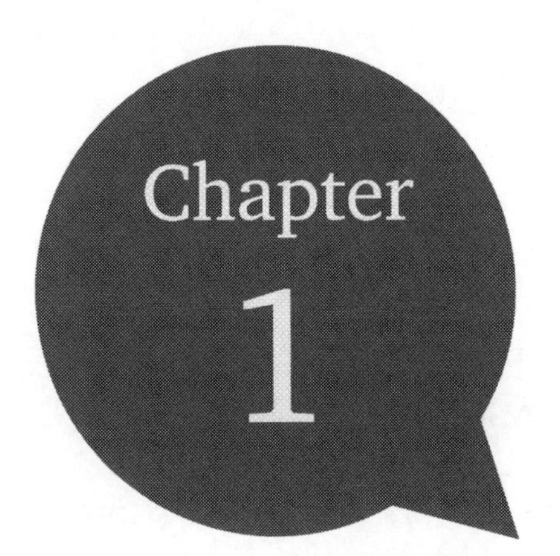

The First Step

> **"The secret of getting ahead is getting started."**
> —Mark Twain (1835-1910), American writer

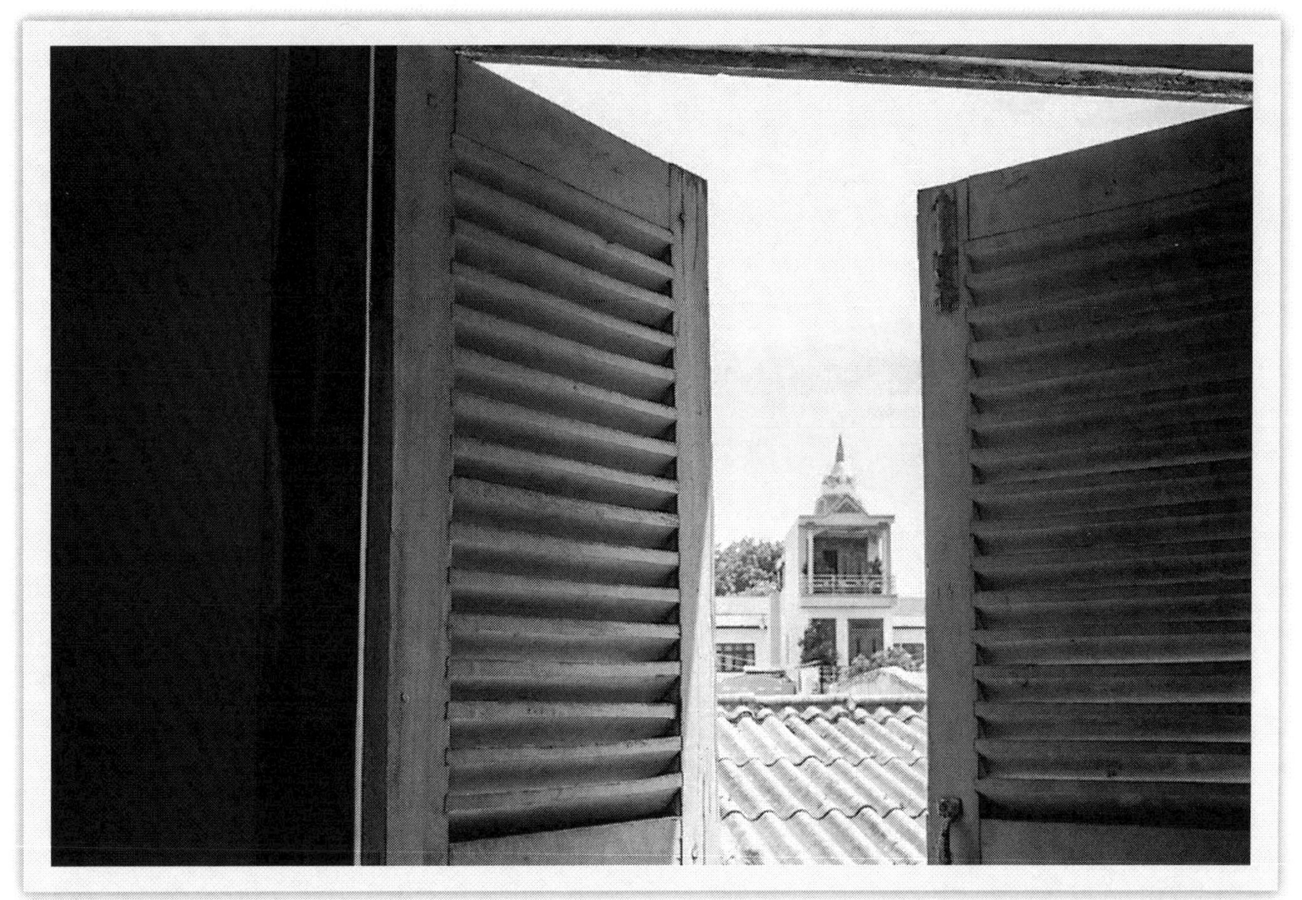

Vince Dang | vincedang.com

Speaking English allows people to express themselves in an international language. In these lessons, you will collaborate with other students by asking and answering questions about your experiences. In these ways, you will be practicing English, learning about other cultures, and finding ways to make conversation pleasant and engaging.

You will also create compelling conversations in English. Have fun!

1 Getting Started

Photographer | Tung Phan

Directions:
Turn the following statements into questions. Walk around the room and ask each person a different question. If they answer "Yes," write their name in the space provided. If the answer is "No," find a different person until your chart is complete or time is called.

Example: Find someone who likes gardening.
"Do you love to garden?"

Find someone who is left handed. ______	Find someone who saw a movie last weekend ______	Find someone who is a stranger to you. ______	Find someone who plays a sport. ______
Find someone who plays a musical instrument. ______	Find someone who likes to sing. ______	Find someone who speaks more than two languages. ______	Find someone who is an only child. ______
Find someone who shops online. ______	Find someone who has caught a fish ______	Find someone who loves to travel. ______	Find someone who has planted a garden ______
Find someone whose first name begins with the same letter as yours. ______	Find someone who was born in the same month as you. ______	Find someone who is wearing the same color shirt as you. ______	Find someone who has two or more siblings. ______

Sharing Experiences

1

Clara Hutzler | www.hellosuitcase.com

Big journeys begin with small steps. In conversation, it is often helpful to show other people that we understand what they wish to communicate. A smile, a nod of the head, and eye contact show that you are interested in what your partner is saying and invite your partner to continue.

Frowning, shaking one's head no, or looking away while others are speaking may discourage them from continuing the conversation. Interrupting, too, may prevent the other person from sharing thoughts. Positive feedback often helps others build confidence.

In this class, we want to encourage each other. Take turns answering the following questions about English. Remember, "A journey of a thousand miles must begin with a single step." (Optional: Write down your partner's answers after asking each question.)

Think About It

What words do you find hard to say in English?

- Why do you want to learn English? Give three reasons.
- To speak English well, how important is it to know something about the western culture?
- What personal qualities do you need to learn a foreign language effectively?
- Is it possible to teach yourself a language?
- Are there some words that are similar in different languages?
- What do you think you can do to improve your English? How can you take your English ability to a higher level?
- What techniques do you have to learn English vocabulary?
- Can you learn a language by watching TV or movies?
- Can a good teacher influence how much you enjoy learning English?
- What dream job would you like to have speaking English in Vietnam?
- What dream job would you like to have speaking English outside of Vietnam?
- What commitments will you make to achieve these dreams?"
- How have those who have learned English become better speakers?
- If you had to teach Vietnamese to a foreigner, what advice would you give them to improve learning Vietnamese?
- What do you know about the TOEFL test? What about the IELTS exam?
- Is there another language you would like to learn? What is it?

1 Word List

Which words do you already know? Underline them, and circle the words you are unsure about. Then review your answers with a partner.

Noun	Verb	Adjective
*conversation /khon.vờ.xây.shần/	agree /ờ.gri/	
courage /khơ.rij/	discourage /đis.cơ.rij/	
gesture /chés.chờ/	argue /ar.gều/	
proverb /pro.vợp/	encourage /in.khơ.rij/	
quotation /khuồ.thây.shần/	disagree /đis.ờ.gri/	
*culture /khu.chờ/	*participate /pàr.thí.xì.pâyt/	

*Indicates words on the Academic Word List. See p.204 for all AWL words used in this book.

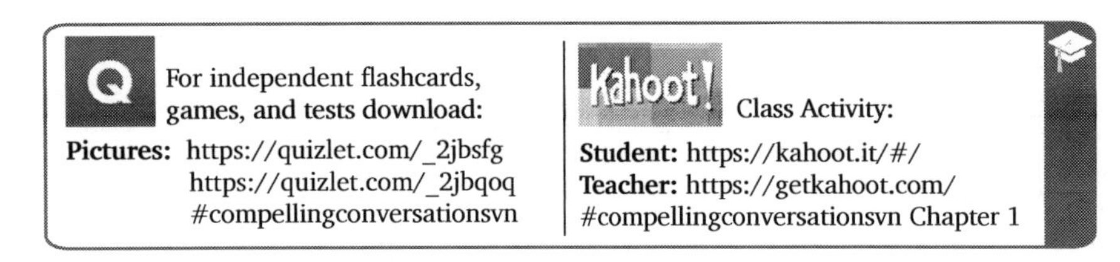

Expanding Vocabulary

Look at the definitions and example sentences below. Do the definitions match what you and your partner expected in the Word List? If not, what is different?

agree [verb]: to think the same way as someone else.

> **Ex:** I **agree** with you.

argue [verb]: to give reasons and strongly disagree.

> **Ex:** Linh **argued** with Nga over the quickest way home in the rain.

1

conversation [noun]: talking; exchanging words between two or more people.

> **Ex:** We have long **conversations** because we can talk about so many topics together.

courage [noun]: bravery, the act of facing danger.

> **Ex:** The little mouse showed a lot of **courage** when he approached the lion.

culture [noun]: the beliefs and values of a particular social, ethnic, or national group.

> **Ex:** American **culture** can be seen in movies, TV shows, and social media posts.

disagree [verb]: to think in a different way; to not agree.

> **Ex:** We **disagree** about the best place to go fishing at night in Vietnam.

discourage [verb]: to make someone feel bad about doing something; to advise against.

> **Ex:** My father **discouraged** me from smoking by explaining how harmful and dangerous it is long-term for my heart, lungs and general health.

encourage [verb]: to make someone feel good about an action; to say "yes, you can."

> **Ex:** The college basketball coach **encourages** all his players to always do their best.

gesture [noun]: a motion or movement of a part of the body.

> **Ex:** Tài bowed his head in a **gesture** of respect and obedience.

participate [verb]: to join in, to take part in something.

> **Ex:** Do you **participate** enough in your college classes?

proverb [noun]: a popular, wise, or traditional saying; a well-known phrase.

> **Ex:** The **proverb** "Actions speak louder than words," means what you do is more important than what you say.

quotation [noun]: a person's exact words; a passage from a book or speech; a famous saying.

> **Ex:** "We have nothing to fear but fear itself," is a famous **quotation** by Franklin D. Roosevelt, the popular 32nd American President.

Grammar Note: Quotation marks (" ") at beginning and end of a sentence or paragraph indicate that it is a direct quotation.

1 Asking Questions with New Vocabulary Words

A. Select five vocabulary words in this chapter and write a question for each word. Remember to start your question with a question word (Who, What, Where, When, Why, How, Is, Are, Do, Did, Does, etc.). You also want to end each question with a question mark (?). Underline each vocabulary word.

Example: *How do you encourage your friends?*

1. ______________________________
2. ______________________________
3. ______________________________
4. ______________________________
5. ______________________________

B. Take turns asking and answering questions with your partner or group members. Ask your instructor to give you feedback on your questions to check your English grammar.

Learning Tips

Here are some tips for building good conversations:

- Be active
- Be curious
- Be encouraging
- Be kind
- Be open
- Be tolerant
- Be yourself

Paraphrasing Proverbs

Proverbs, or traditional sayings, can show big ideas in a few words. We will use proverbs and famous quotations so we can look at the ideas of many people and cultures and discuss these ideas. We will also often paraphrase, or put into other words, proverbs and discuss quotations to expand our vocabulary.

Paraphrasing is an important skill in both writing and speaking. In this exercise, take turns reading the proverbs out loud. What does each sentence mean? As a group, paraphrase the proverb by using different words to show the same idea. Remember to encourage each other with words and gestures.

Vietnamese:

Words don't cost money to buy; choose your words carefully to please each other.
"Lời nói chẳng mất tiền mua, lựa lời mà nói cho vừa lòng nhau."
Meaning: ______________________________

As a person we have a mouth and lips; why does she speak like a pot with no lid.
"Làm người có miệng có môi, sao cô căm cắm như nồi không vung."
Meaning: ____________________

Keep the words you say; do not be like the butterflies: land and then leave.
"Nói lời phải giữ lấy lời, đừng như con bướm đậu rồi lại bay."
Meaning: ____________________

International:

You catch more flies with honey than with vinegar. —English
Meaning: ____________________

I hear and I forget. I see and I remember. I do and I understand. —Chinese
Meaning: ____________________

We learn by doing. —English
Meaning: ____________________

You know enough if you know how to learn. —Greek
Meaning: ____________________

Keep it light, bright and polite. —English
Meaning: ____________________

The Conversation Continues

Sharing English Conversation Tips

With the other members in your group, make a list of five important rules to follow which will help you create pleasant conversations.

Example: *Keep eye contact with conversation partners.*

1. ____________________
2. ____________________
3. ____________________
4. ____________________
5. ____________________

"Do what you can, with what you have, where you are."
—Theodore Roosevelt (1858-1919), 26th U.S. President

1 Building Words

Adding the Latin Prefix "dis-"

We can build a strong vocabulary with a few simple techniques. We can also make new vocabulary words by adding a few letters to the beginning of the vocabulary word. These letters are known as a "prefix". This powerful technique allows us to build our active vocabulary and to help us recognize unfamiliar vocabulary words.

Prefix	Meaning	Example
dis-	not, opposite	Friends often agree on many topics, but sometimes they "**dis**agree" and see things in different and even opposite ways.
dis-	apart, away from	The floods "**dis**placed" many families as the sudden rush of water destroyed many homes and forced people away from the area.

Complete the chart below by following the example. For the last two rows, add new base words.

Prefix	Base	New Word
dis-	agree	*disagree*
dis-	courage	
dis-	connect	
dis-	play	
dis-	place	
dis-	able	
dis-	ability	
dis-	grace	
dis-	trust	
dis-		
dis-		

1

A. Select four words from the above chart and create a question for your partner. Remember to start your question with a question word (Who, What, Where, When, Why, How, Is, Are, Do, Did, Does, etc.). You also want to end each question with a question mark (?). Underline each vocabulary word.

1. ______________________________
2. ______________________________
3. ______________________________
4. ______________________________

B. Take turns asking and answering questions with your partner. Ask your instructor to give you feedback on your questions to check your English grammar.

Discussing Quotations

Quotations appear throughout this book. Reading the ideas of other intelligent people from different era and different cultures provides a larger perspective. It also emphasizes how some compelling conversations have continued across the centuries and across continents. Finally, quotations can demonstrate clear language and build cultural knowledge.

In your small group, read aloud each of the following quotations. Decide among yourselves what you think the quotation means. Then, discuss how the meaning of the quotation will help you work well with other students in this class. Remember to practice using encouraging gestures and words with each other.

1. **"Courtesy costs nothing."**
   —Ralph Waldo Emerson (1803–1882), American writer, philosopher

2. **"I never know how much of what I say is true."**
   —Bette Midler (1945–), American singer, actress

3. **"The secret of education is respecting the pupil."**
   —Ralph Waldo Emerson (1803–1882), American poet, philosopher

4. **"It is not best that we should all think alike; it is a difference of opinion which makes horse races."**
   —Mark Twain (1835–1910), American writer, humorist

5. **"I am tomorrow, or some future day, what I establish today. I am today what I established yesterday or some previous day."**
   —James Joyce (1882–1941), Irish novelist

1

Discussion: Which was your favorite quote? Why?

____

____

____

Let's continue reading some more quotations out loud and discussing them in small groups. Do you agree with the quotation? Disagree? Why? Mark your opinion. Afterwards, pick a favorite quotation. Remember to give a reason or an example.

1. **"All great speakers were bad speakers first."**
   —Ralph Waldo Emerson (1803–1882), American poet ☐**Agree** ☐**Disagree**

2. **"Speech is civilization itself…It is silence which isolates."**
   —Thomas Mann (1875–1955), German writer ☐**Agree** ☐**Disagree**

3. **"If it is language that makes us human, one half of language is to listen."**
   —Jacob Trapp (1899–1992), American orator ☐**Agree** ☐**Disagree**

4. **"Man does not speak because he thinks; he thinks because he speaks. Or rather, speaking is no different than thinking: to speak is to think."**
   —Octavio Paz, (1914–1998), Mexican writer, Nobel Prize winner ☐**Agree** ☐**Disagree**

5. **"Life shrinks or expands in proportion to one's courage."**
   —Anaïs Nin (1903–1977), French-American author ☐**Agree** ☐**Disagree**

Discussion: Which was your favorite quote? Why?

____

____

____

Pronunciation Corner

Some English students make learning English more difficult by expecting themselves to be perfect and speak exactly like a native English speaker. That's a noble, but very, very difficult goal.

For now, a more important goal is to speak in a clear, natural way so your listeners can understand your words and ideas. Remember that English speakers also have many different accents—especially in the United States. Therefore, we will focus much more on natural, clear speech than perfect pronunciation. Being understood matters most.

However, using a few techniques will often improve your English pronunciation:

1. **Open the mouth wider.** In English you will need to make (or use) a lot more air than in speaking Vietnamese.
2. **Speak slower to pronounce all syllables.** English words often have more than one syllable.
3. **Pay attention to word endings.** In English, they can change the meaning of a word. The Vietnamese language, in contrast, does not use word endings, known as suffixes, as clues to the meaning or form of words.

Feel free to ask your partner to repeat a word or sentence if you do not understand. Americans do this all the time if they do not understand a question.

Pair work: Here is a list of helpful phrases to help you when you need to ask for clarification or understanding. Take turns saying the expressions.

To ask the other person to say it again, but in a different way:

- Could you put it differently, please?
  /Khúd du pút ít đíph.phận.lì?/
- I wonder if you could say that in a different way.
  /Ai woanh.đớ ìph du khúd xêy đát in ờ đíph.phận wuê?/

To ask the other person to repeat:

- Could you say that again, please?
  /Khúd du xêy đát ớ.ghên, plíz?/
- Sorry, could you repeat please?
  /So.rì, khúd du rì.pít, plíz?/
- Would you mind repeating that please?
  /Wật du mai.d rì.pít.thìng đát, plíz?/

To ask the other person to slow down:

- I'm sorry, but would you speak slowly please.
  /Ai.m so.rì, bật wật du spík slâu.lì plíz./
- Can you please speak slower?
  /Khèn du plíz spík slâu.ờ?/

1

To ask for a definition:

- Do you mean...?
  /Đù yu min…?/
- Sorry, I don't quite understand. What does "…" mean?
  /So.rì, ai độn.t khoai.t ân.đờ.sten. Wắt đơz "…" min?/

To say you don't understand:

- I beg your pardon, but I don't quite understand.
  /Ai be.g dò po.đần, bật ai độn.t khoai.t ân.đờ.sten./
- I beg your pardon?
  /Ai be.g dò po.đần?/
- I don't quite see what you mean.
  /Ai độn.t khoai.t xi wắt du min./
- I don't quite see what you're getting at.
  /Ai độn.t khoai.t xi wắt dờ két.đing ạt./
- Sorry, I didn't get your point.
  /So.rì, ai điết.đận két. dờ poi.th./

To ask the other person to speak louder:

- Sorry, I didn't quite hear what you said.
  /So.rì, ai điết.đận khoai.t hia wắt du xéđ./
- I'm sorry, can you speak a bit louder?
  /Ai.m so.rì, khèn du plíz spík ờ bít lao.đờ?/

"Nothing in life is to be feared. It is only to be understood."
—Marie Curie (1867-1934), physicist

Culture Corner

Shaking Hands

In western cultures, handshakes are a formal and common way of greeting others. Have you ever wondered where this originated?

Some scholars believe the tradition began during Medieval times. At that time, European men were covered in heavy armor that limited movement, so handshakes were intended to express friendliness. This greeting was either received with the same extended open hand gesture to indicate friendship or a sword to show hostility.

As a result, a firm handshake has become the standard of politeness when first meeting someone, the opposite gender included. For better or for worse, many Americans believe that how you handshake shows your character. Therefore, you want to have a firm handshake to make a positive first impression.

How to Handshake:

1. During the greeting, make eye contact with your acquaintance and smile while extending your right hand at waist level with your thumb up and palm flat.
2. Grasp the other person's hand using a firm grip, palm on palm and your thumb pointed at a 45° angle.
3. Keep in mind that handshakes are firm, brief, and confident.
4. Introduce yourself. "I'm Susan" or "Jack."
5. Say "How do you do?" or "Good to meet you."

Things to Avoid:

- Shaking the hand (up and down) more than three times. You want to keep it short and firm.
- Applying so much pressure in the squeeze that there is pain on the other person's face.
- Applying too little pressure – you don't want your hands to be like "a dead fish."

Activity 1: In small groups, walk around the class, shake hands with your classmates, and introduce yourselves.

Activity 2: With a partner, discuss how the following groups typically greet each other in your country.

Clara Hutzler | www.hellosuitcase.com

- How do adult men greet each other?
- How do adult men greet adult women?
- How do adult men greet younger people (teenagers or children)?
- How do adult women greet each other?
- How do adult women greet younger people (teenagers or children)?
- How do teenage boys greet each other?
- How do teenage boys greet teenage girls?
- How do teenage girls greet each other?
- How do teachers greet students?
- How do store clerks greet their customers?

1 Classroom Extention

Speech Observations

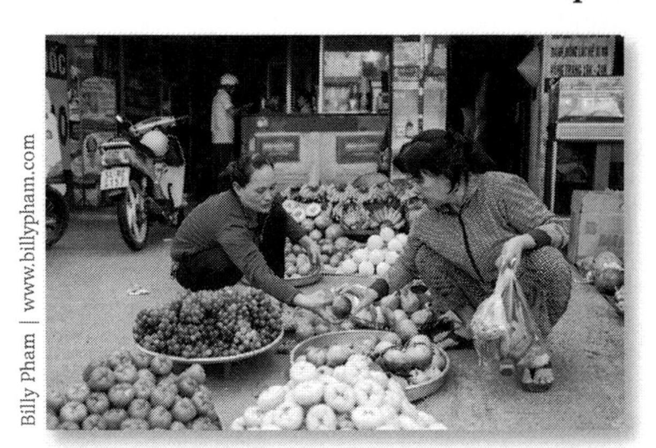

Billy Pham | www.billypham.com

People communicate with words 24 hours a day, seven days a week. During the next 24 hours, carefully observe people talking to each other.

Note their communication style, gestures, and word choices. You can watch people in stores, on buses, at school and even on TV.

Some questions to think about while observing:

1. What facial expressions are they making? Where are their eyes focusing?
2. What hand gestures are being used? How is the body positioned? What mannerism and habitual purposeful movement are they making?
3. What is the energy level? Are they enjoying the conversation?
4. Does their communication inspire emotion in the listener?
5. How is the speech pattern? Are there pauses?

Prepare to share these observations with the class:

	Facial Expression	**Body Language**	**Vocal Expression**
At the supermarket			

> **"The strength of the nation derives from the integrity of the home."**
> —Confucius (551-479 B.C.E), Chinese philosopher

Search & Share

Reviewing Pronunciation Tips on the Internet

Student Name:____________________ Date:____________________

Find a video on the Internet that gives tips or suggestions on improving English pronunciation. Look for ways to be better understood in English. You can search for common word stress patterns in English. Watch the video, listen carefully, take notes, and share the pronunciation tips with your classmates.

Video Title:____________________ Length:____________________

Web Address:____________________ Creator:____________________

1. Describe the video.
2. What pronunciation tips did the video give?
3. Which words or sounds did the video focus on?
4. How practical did you find the advice? Why?
5. What was the strongest part? Why?
6. What was the weakest part? Why?
7. Who do you think is the target audience for this video? Why?
8. Why did you choose this video?
9. Do you think this video will help improve your pronunciation of English words?
10. How would you rate this video on a scale of 1–5, with 5 being the highest? Why?

> **"I was the kind nobody thought could make it. I had a funny Boston accent. I couldn't pronounce my R's. I wasn't a beauty."**
> —Barbara Walters (1929–), American television journalist

Beyond Hello

"Everything becomes a little different as soon as it is spoken out loud."
—Hermann Hesse (1877-1962), German novelist and Nobel Prize winner

Getting Started

Speed Dating

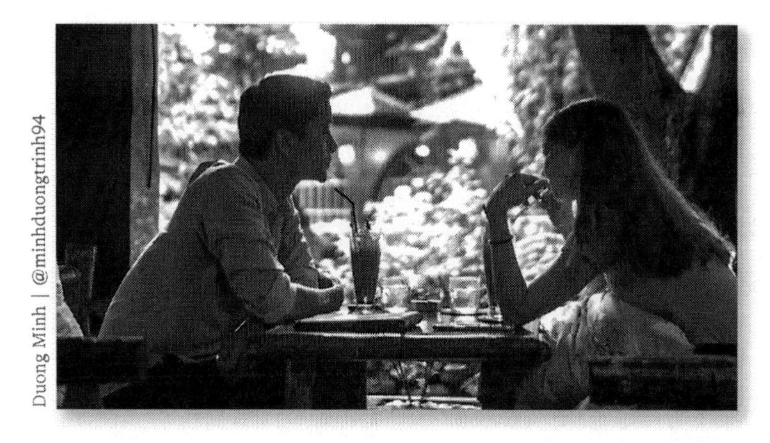
Duong Minh | @minhduongtrinh94

Directions:
Let's learn more about our classmates. Depending on your instructor, you will rotate to have a few minutes with each classmate. During this time, ask the person sitting across from you the list of questions below and she will do the same to you. Feel free to add or omit any questions.

Teacher: Countdown timer: http://www.online-stopwatch.

Speed Dating Questions:

1. What's your full name? How do you spell that?
2. Where did you grow up?
3. Is that a city, village, or suburb?
4. Are you the first child? Second? Fifth?
5. What do you like to do in your free time?

Sharing Experiences

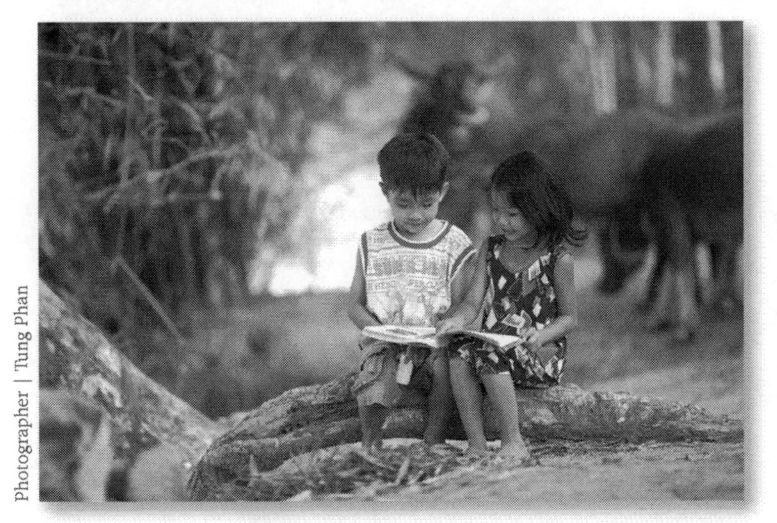

Photographer | Tung Phan

Interview the person sitting next to you. Take turns talking, write notes, and prepare to introduce your partner to our class. Feel free to add or omit any questions that you want. Challenge yourself by speaking full sentences instead of short, one-word answers. Let's begin!

1. Do you have any older brothers? Sisters? Younger siblings?
2. Who chose your name? Why?
3. How would you describe yourself as a child? Why? Do you mean...?
4. Did you have a favorite toy? Other possession? Why?
5. Do you have a favorite possession today? What?
6. Do you have a favorite color?
7. What's your favorite season? Why?
8. Do you have a favorite number? What? Can you guess why?
9. Do you have any pets? What is your pet's name?
10. What's your favorite animal?
11. What kind of music do you listen to?
12. Do you have a favorite singer? Group?
13. What's your favorite radio station or television channel? Why?
14. What movies can you recommend?
15. Why do you like those films?

Word List

Which words do you already know? Underline them, and circle the words you are unsure about. Then review your answers with a partner.

Noun	Verb	Adjective
impression /ìm.presh.shần/	*appreciate /ờ.pri.sì.ệt/	
enthusiasm /ìn.tu.gì.a.dầm/	**interview** **/in.thờ.vêu/**	
frown **/phraon/**	**frown** **/phraon/**	
interview **/in.thờ.vêu/**	recommend /réc.cờ.men/	
possession /pờ.zes.shần/	*cooperate /khồ.óp.bờ.rệt/	
*goal /gôl/	*interact /in.thờ.ác shần/	
sibling /síb.bling/	**smile** /smai.ồ/	
smile **/smai.ồ/**		

*Indicates words on the Academic Word List. See p.204 for all AWL words used in this book.

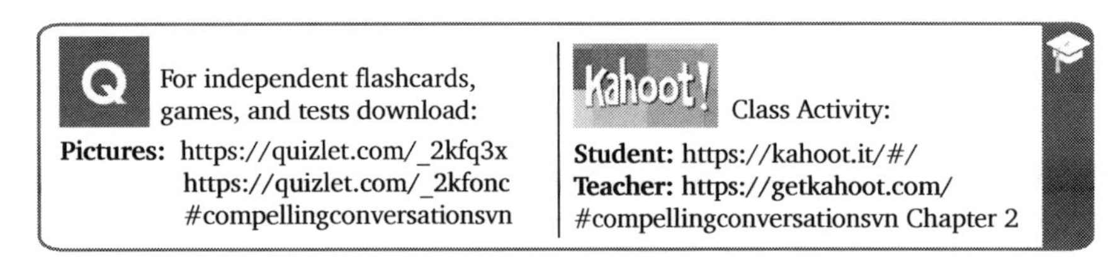

Expanding Vocabulary

Look at the definitions and example sentences below. Do the definitions match what you and your partner expected in the Word List? If not, what is different?

appreciate [verb]: to feel thankful for something, to like and see the value in something.

> **Ex:** She **appreciates** your friendship.

cooperate [verb]: to work together.

> **Ex:** Let's **cooperate** and help each other learn more English words in this class!

enthusiasm [noun]: excitement; a passion for someone or something.

> Ex: He showed his **enthusiasm** by loudly cheering for the local sports team.

2

frown [noun]: a sad or disapproving where the mouth widens downward at both ends.
[verb]: to show unhappiness or displeasure with the face; the opposite of smile.

> Ex: Her **frown** showed her displeasure with her poor test results.
> She **frowned** in the mirror, but smiled when she saw her best.

goal [noun]: a target, a desired result.

> Ex: The **goal** is to get at least 100 on the TOEFL exam.

impression [noun]: a mental "picture" left by a person, place, or thing in the mind.

> Ex: Make a good **impression** on your supervisor if you want a better job.

interact [verb]: meet and act on each other.

> Ex: We will **interact** with each other in many speaking activities this semester.

interview [noun]: a formal conversation.
[verb]: to systematically ask questions.

> Ex: My job **interview** lasted 20 minutes, and the manager wants to **interview** me again next week.

possession [noun]: holding or owning an object.

> Ex: Her favorite **possession** is a ring that her grandmother gave her years ago.

recommend [verb]: to advise, to give your opinion.

> Ex: I **recommend** you try the delicious shrimp soup.

sibling [noun]: brother or sister in the same family.

> Ex: I have two **siblings**: a younger brother and an older sister.

smile [noun]: an expression of happiness where the mouth widens upward at both ends.
[verb]: to display happiness or pleasure with the face — the opposite of frown.

> Ex: Bảo Châu has a wonderful **smile**!
> Kiều Anh **smiles** so broadly you can see all her teeth.

Asking Questions with New Vocabulary Words

2

A. Select five vocabulary words in this chapter and write a question for each word. Remember to start your question with a question word (Who, What, Where, When, Why, How, Is, Are, Do, Did, Does, etc.). You also want to end each question with a question mark (?). Underline each vocabulary word.

Example: *Can you recommend a good book?*

1. ______________________________
2. ______________________________
3. ______________________________
4. ______________________________
5. ______________________________

B. Take turns asking and answering questions with your partner or group members. Ask your instructor to give you feedback on your questions to check your English grammar.

Paraphrasing Proverbs

Read the following proverbs and discuss them with your partner. Write what you think they mean in the spaces provided. Circle your favorites. Explain your choices.

Vietnamese:

Which person would use a gold needle to make a fishing net? Which wise person would speak harshly to each other?
"Kim vàng ai nỡ uốn câu. Người khôn ai nỡ nói nhau nặng lời."
Meaning: ______________________________

The first love is a ponytail. The second love is speaking in a sweet, charming manner.
"Một thương tóc bỏ đuôi gà. Hai thương ăn nói mặn mà, có duyên."
Meaning: ______________________________

A sentence not said is nine good sentences.
"Một câu nhịn, chín câu lành."
Meaning: ______________________________

International:

Strangers are just friends you haven't met yet. —American
Meaning: ____________________

Beauty is a good letter of recommendation. —German
Meaning: ____________________

You never get a second chance to make a first impression. —American
Meaning: ____________________

You're never too old to learn. —Latin
Meaning: ____________________

A single conversation across the table with a wise person is worth a month's study of books. —Chinese
Meaning: ____________________

Building Words

Adding the Latin Suffix "-ion"

We can also make a new vocabulary word by adding a few letters to the end of others we already know. These letters are known as a "suffix". This powerful technique allows us to build our vocabulary and to help us recognize unfamiliar vocabulary words.

Suffix	Meaning	Example
-ion	condition	"Apprecia**tion**" is a condition. We feel "apprecia**tion**" when our hard work is recognized, and this condition is a positive one.
-ion	action	"Participa**tion**" is an action. Getting an excellent grade in our English class requires your active "participa**tion**!"

2

Complete the chart below by following the example. For the last two rows, add new base words.

Verb	Suffix	New Noun
impress	-ion	*impression*
elect	-ion	
possess	-ion	
construct	-ion	
deduct	-ion	
	-ion	
	-ion	

The Drop "e" Rule: We usually drop the "e" at the end of root words when we add a suffix that begins with a vowel.

Follow this pattern to complete the chart below by changing the verb into a noun.

Verb	Suffix	New Noun
contribute	-ion	*contribution*
celebrate	-ion	
generate	-ion	
appreciate	-ion	
locate	-ion	
note	-ion	
participate	-ion	
create	-ion	

A. Select four words from the above chart and create a question for your partner. Remember to start your question with a question word (Who, What, Where, When, Why, How, Is, Are, Do, Did, Does, etc.). You also want to end each question with a question mark (?). Underline each vocabulary word. Get feedback on your questions to check your English grammar.

1. ______________________________
2. ______________________________
3. ______________________________
4. ______________________________

B. Take turns asking and answering questions with your partner.

2

Discussing Quotations

In your small groups, take turns reading these quotations out loud and discuss them. Do you agree with the quotation? Disagree? Why? Mark your opinion. Afterwards, pick a favorite quotation. Remember to give a reason or an example.

1. **"I never met a man I didn't like."**
   —Will Rogers (1879–1935), American ☐ **Agree** ☐ **Disagree**

2. **"I am free of all prejudices. I hate every one equally."**
   —W. C. Fields (1880–1946), American actor/comedian ☐ **Agree** ☐ **Disagree**

3. **"There is no such thing as a worthless conversation, provided you know what to listen for. And questions are the breath of life for a conversation."**
   —James Nathan Miller (1953–), American journalist ☐ **Agree** ☐ **Disagree**

4. **"Conversation is an art in which a man has all mankind for his competitors, for it is that which all are practicing every day while they live."**
   —Ralph Waldo Emerson (1803–1882), American essayist ☐ **Agree** ☐ **Disagree**

5. **"The true spirit of conversation consists in building on another man's observation, not overturning it."**
   —Edward G. Bulwer-Lytton (1803–1873), British novelist ☐ **Agree** ☐ **Disagree**

6. **"Confidence contributes more to conversation than wit."**
   —Francois de La Rochefoucauld (1613–1680), French writer ☐ **Agree** ☐ **Disagree**

7. **"It takes two to speak truth—one to speak and another to hear."**
   —Henry David Thoreau (1817–1862), American writer ☐ **Agree** ☐ **Disagree**

8. **"I am simple, complex, generous, selfish, unattractive, beautiful, lazy and driven."**
   —Barbara Streisand (1942–), American singer/actress ☐ **Agree** ☐ **Disagree**

9. **"It was impossible to get a conversation going; every body was talking too much**
   —Yogi Berra (1925–), legendary baseball manager ☐ **Agree** ☐ **Disagree**

10. "Never let your fear of striking out get in your way."
—Babe Ruth (1895–1948), American baseball legend ☐ **Agree** ☐ **Disagree**

Discussion: Which was your favorite quote? Why?

The Conversation Continues

Clara Hutzler | www.hellosuitcase.com

Let's continue to explore topics beyond saying hello with one or two classmates. Use complete sentences to respond.

1. What do you like to do outside? Why?
2. Where do you go to walk or jog?
3. What is your favorite sport? Why?
4. When is your free time?
5. How do you like to spend your free time? What interests you?
6. Do you have a hobby? Do you collect anything? How long have you enjoyed it?
7. How long have you studied English? Where?

8. What makes you smile? Where do you feel most comfortable?
9. What are some things that might cause you to frown?
10. Have you ever been interviewed before? If so, why?
11. Do you have a favorite English or Vietnamese word or expression? Why?
12. What are your goals for this year? Why?
13. What is your plan to reach your goals?
14. How would your friends describe you? What would you add?
15. What are three things that you appreciate about living in Vietnam?

My Goals

Places I want to speak English:

____
____
____
____
____

Pronunciation Corner

Syllables

Syllables are the basic units of rhythm in a word. Remember that Vietnamese is a monosyllabic language, meaning there is only one syllable per word. On the other hand, English words often have many syllables.

Pair work: **How many syllables?**

Student A: Say one word from a column below. You can choose a word from column 1, 2, 3, 4, or 5.

Student B: Hold up one finger if the word has one syllable, two fingers if the word has two syllables, etc…

When you get five correct in a row, switch roles. Circle the words that were trickiest for you so that you can practice.

2

1 Syllable	2 Syllables	3 Syllables	4 Syllables	5 Syllables
boss	teacher	butterfly	alligator	alphabetical
call	rabbit	elephant	helicopter	anniversary
clap	paper	computer	caterpillar	cafeteria
close	table	umbrella	watermelon	communication
flow	pencil	hamburger	anybody	congratulations
lime	candy	dinosaur	apologize	cooperation
one	slipper	bicycle	appreciate	denominator
paint	window	basketball	calculator	disagreeable
peace	apple	broccoli	celebration	electricity
red	monkey	dishwasher	discovery	hippopotamus
rose	rocket	strawberry	elevator	imagination
run	tiger	potato	impossible	mathematical
school	glasses	octopus	invisible	personality
sleep	spider	telephone	librarian	refrigerator
sport	zebra	microwave	obedient	unforgettable
state	doctor	grasshopper	questionable	university
sun	garden	piano	supermarket	unquestionable
top	number	president	television	vocabulary

Culture Corner

What's in a Name?

Billy Pham | www.billypham.com

Americans generally have three parts in their name:

- The surname (family name) which is called the "last name."
- The given name which is called the "first name."
- And some people, not all, have a "middle name" or "middle initial" in addition.

In most situations, the first name appears first, then the middle name or initial, and then the last name.

Example: John (first) Fitzgerald (middle) Kennedy (Last)

However, on a majority of applications and forms, the last name is listed first, followed by a comma, and then the first name and middle initial.

2

Example: Kennedy (last), John (first) F. (middle)

If your name is unusual in American culture (e.g. Ngọc), be patient while other people learn how to pronounce your name correctly: there are sounds in your name that are uncommon in the English language. Some people will choose an "Americanized" version of their name to make it easier for others to pronounce and/or remember, but this option remains a personal choice.

Many Americans enjoy using a nickname, or causal name, among friends. Some people will insist that you call them by their nickname if they have one. If your name is long and difficult to pronounce, your friends or classmates may give you a nickname that could be a shorter, easier version of your own name (e.g. "Tim" short for "Timothy"). Nicknames are usually used among friends to show affection or friendliness.

Billy Pham | www.billypham.com

Activity:

Do you have a nickname? Would you like to have one? What nickname would you like for yourself? With a partner, discuss why you chose some possible nicknames.

____

____

____

____

____

____

____

"Accept me as I am—only then will we discover each other."
—Federico Fellini (1920-1993), Italian director/screenwriter

Classroom Activity: Role-Play

2

What's your expression?

Superb conversation skills require facial expressions, body language, and vocal expressions. Look at each expression below. With a partner, decide which feeling is being expressed in each picture (e.g. mysterious, excited, angry, surprised, etc…).

A. Facial Expression

Option A: With a partner, take turns choosing a feeling from the list below and express it on your face. Make sure to not tell your partner which feeling you are choosing. Your partner should be able to guess which feeling you are expressing. If your partner is unable to guess, exaggerate the feeling until he is able to. Do this for each feeling below.

Photographer | Kim Ngo

Option B: Using a smart device, take a selfie of yourself expressing the feelings from the list below. Take a look at your photos. You should be able to name the feeling that is being expressed. If not, keep taking the photos until you're able to. Walk around the class and have other classmates guess the feeling you're expressing.

1. Mysterious
2. Bored
3. Excited
4. Surprised
5. Heartbroken
6. Nervous

B. Body Language

Discuss with your partner what body language you could add to make your expressions better. Try again to copy one of the facial expressions, but add hand gestures and/or body language. You will see that it'll be easier for your partner to guess what feeling you're expressing!

C. Vocal Expression

Option A: With a partner, say each sentence below using a different feeling given. Express the feeling using only the tone of your voice.

Option B: Using your smart device, voice record yourself saying each sentence below using a different feeling given. Express the feeling using only the tone of your voice. Listen to your recordings. You should be able to name the feeling that is being expressed. If not, keep voice recording until you're able to. Walk around the class and have other classmates guess the feeling you're expressing.

1. "How many times have you been lost?" (surprised, sad)
2. "It's raining." (bored, joyful)
3. "You think so?" (doubtful, angry)

Search & Share

Watching the News

Student Name:____________________________ Date:____________________________

"Search and Share" exercises ask you to find information on your own and bring the information back to your classmates to discuss in small groups. This homework exercise helps you to use real English materials and bring your voice into the classroom.

For homework, watch a news report in your best language for 5-10 minutes. You can use the TV or the Internet to find a video in which a news announcer is sitting in the studio presenting the news.

First watch the news with the sound "muted," or with the volume turned all the way down, so you can focus on the presenter's body language. As you watch, look at the speaker's face (especially on the mouth) and on the speaker's hand and body movements.

Video (non-English):____

Source:__________________________________ Topic:________________________

Captions/Descriptions:____

Next, find another 5-10 minute news report on TV or on the Internet in English. Like before, watch it with the volume as low as possible or on the "mute" setting. While you watch, again pay close attention to the person's mouth, face, hands, and gestures.

Video (non-English):____

Source:__________________________________ Topic:________________________

Captions/Descriptions:____

Describe the person speaking your best language. Describe the person speaking English. Was the mouth of either announcer open wide more often? What did you notice about the person's face or hands? What else did you see? What do you think this means? Why?

> **"The body never lies."**
> —Martha Graham (1894-1991), American dancer and choreographer

School and Knowledge

"Education is the most powerful weapon which you can use to change the world."
—Nelson Mandela (1918-2013), South African President

Photographer | Tung Phan

Getting Started

3

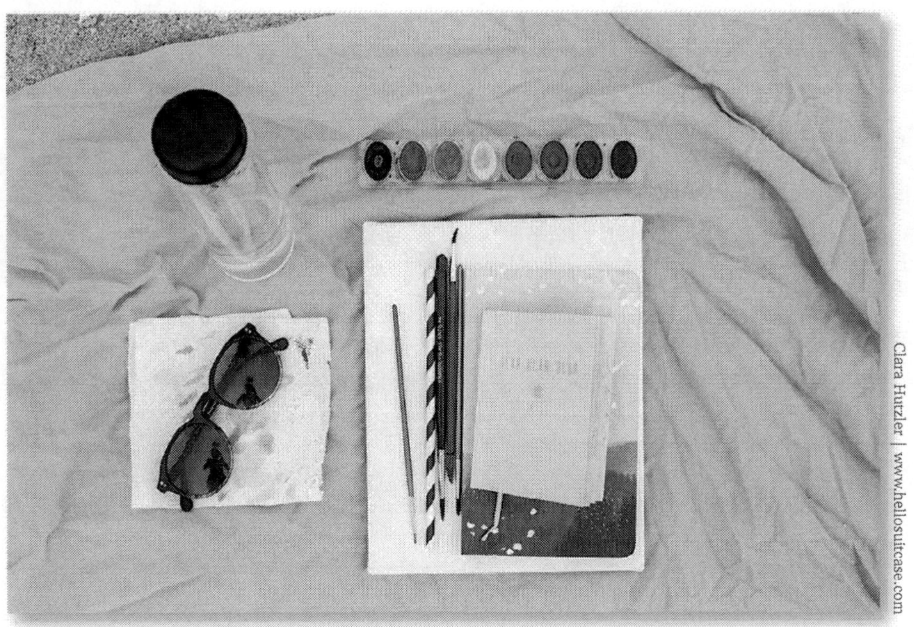

Clara Hutzler | www.hellosuitcase.com

Directions:
List as many items as possible. After a few minutes, compare your lists with your partner.

Nouns	Verbs	Adjectives
Things found at school.	Activities done at school.	Ways to describe your school.

Sharing Experiences

3

Donovan Bui | www.donovanbui.com

We have spent thousands of hours in schools, learned many skills, and collected numerous stories. Many people have positive, fond memories from years in school. Share your fondest school stories with a classmate.

1. Approximately how many hours a week were you in school? Did you go to school on Saturdays?
2. How did you usually get to school? Did you walk, take a bus, ride a bike, or use another form of transportation?
3. How many students were in your class? Was that too few, too many, or just right?
4. Can you describe the feeling, or the atmosphere, in your school?
5. What was the name of your elementary school? High school?
6. Did you attend a public or private school? Why?
7. Was there a school dress code? What were some other rules?
8. How would you describe your elementary school? Did you enjoy it?
9. Were your parents involved in your studies? How?
10. How were your grades? How would you describe yourself as a student?
11. Can you describe the classroom conditions in your high school?
12. What subjects did you take in high school? What were your options? Did you choose your courses?
13. What was your favorite course? Why?
14. Were there any classes that you feared or hated? Why?
15. Did you have to take standardized exams? Which exam was the most difficult? Why?

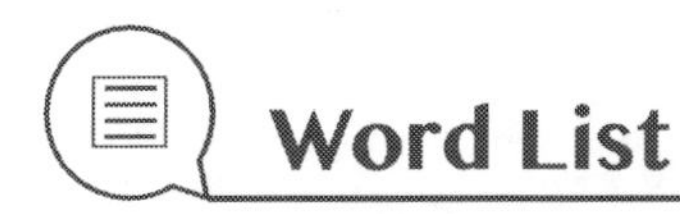

Word List

Which words do you already know? Underline them, and circle the words you are unsure about. Then review your answers with a partner.

3

Noun	Verb	Adjective
adversity /ạt.vơ.si.đì/	**bully** **/bu.lì/**	*academic /ác.ca.đe.mịc/
bully **/bu.lì/**	**mentor** **/men.thờ/**	elementary /e.le.men.trì/
dormitory /đom.mơ.tho.rì/	**tutor** **/thu.thờ/**	
dress code /jes.khôd/	*achieve /ờ.chív/	
fieldtrip /phil.chịp/	***lecture** **/léc.chờ/**	
mentor **/men.thờ/**		
tutor **/thu.thờ/**		
***lecture** **/léc.chờ/**		

*Indicates words on the Academic Word List. See p.204 for all AWL words used in this book.

Expanding Vocabulary

Look at the definitions and example sentences below. Do the definitions match what you and your partner expected in the Word List? If not, what is different?

academic [adjective]: educational, related to school.

> Ex: **Academic** life offers many emotional and intellectual rewards to teachers, but fewer financial ones than some other "white collar" professions.

3

achieve [verb]: to get by effort, or to gain.

> Ex: Bảo Định **achieved** his goal and earned a place on the Dean's List again!

adversity [noun]: harsh conditions, suffering; bad luck or hardship.

> Ex: **Adversity** sometimes makes people and nations stronger as they learn to solve problems and overcome obstacles.

bully [noun]: an aggressive person who threatens schoolmates.
[verb]: to scare or threaten a person.

> Ex: **Bullies** must be disciplined by school authorities.
> No one can **bully** a strong woman.

campus [noun]: school grounds.

> Ex: The **campus** remains the center of academic life at many universities.

dormitory [noun]: a building where college students live and sleep.

> Ex: The new **dormitory** includes air conditioning, large kitchens, and an indoor swimming pool.

dress code [noun]: rules about what clothing is allowed in school.

> Ex: The school **dress code** prohibits short skirts.

elementary [adjective]: primary, basic; fundamental.

> Ex: **Elementary** school begins with kindergarten.

field trip [noun]: an organized trip a class takes away from campus.

> Ex: We took several **field trips** to both local and national museums.

lecture [noun]: a speech given before a class.
[verb]: to give a verbal rebuke; to tell someone that they have done wrong.

> Ex: Have you heard Dr. Quỳnh's **lecture** on learning new English words?
> Many parents **lecture** their children to study hard and get excellent grades.

mentor [noun]: a person to admire or imitate; one who sets a good example and helps a younger, less experienced student or co-worker.

> Ex: My father is a great role model and **mentor**.

tutor [noun]: a private teacher who helps a student outside of class.

> Ex: My TOEFL **tutor** gave me extra help with my English lessons after school.

3

Asking Questions with New Vocabulary Words

A. Select five vocabulary words in this chapter and write a question for each word. Remember to start your question with a question word (Who, What, Where, When, Why, How, Is, Are, Do, Did, Does, etc.). You also want to end each question with a question mark (?). Underline each vocabulary word.

Example: *Where is the school campus?*

1. ______________________________
2. ______________________________
3. ______________________________
4. ______________________________
5. ______________________________

B. Take turns asking and answering questions with your partner or group. Ask your instructor to give you feedback on your questions to check your English grammar.

Remember

- Study hard.
- Remain curious.
- Do your best.

Paraphrasing Proverbs

Read the following proverbs and discuss them with your partner. Write what you think they mean in the spaces provided. Circle your favorites. Explain your choices.

Vietnamese:

One day of travelling broadens the mind.
"Đi một ngày đàng học một sàng khôn."
Meaning: ______________________________

Learning from a friend is better than learning from a teacher.
"Học thầy không tày học bạn."
Meaning: ______

First is manners, second is knowledge.
"Tiên học lễ, hậu học văn."
Meaning: ______

3

International:

Learning colors a man more than the deepest dye. —Chinese
Meaning: ______

A dog near a school will learn to recite lessons in three years. —Korean
Meaning: ______

He who is afraid to ask is ashamed of learning. —Danish
Meaning: ______

We learn to walk by stumbling. —Bulgarian
Meaning: ______

Don't step on your teacher's shadow. —Korean
Meaning: ______

Building Words

Adding the Greek Suffix "-logy"

What academic subjects are you interested in? What areas of special knowledge do you have? The Greek suffix "logy" means "area of knowledge." Let's see if you can put together some new words with this suffix.

Suffix	Meaning	Example
-logy	area of knowledge, study of	The word "archaeo**logy**" means the study of ancient (human) history. We can logically find many popular college majors end in this suffix. Sometimes people use the suffix "ology" too.
-logy	something said	An "apology" is something said to express regret. "Tira apologized for being late again." Although it is odd, "apo**logy**" can also be used to defend something. Plato wrote "The Apo**logy**" to defend the Greek philosopher Socrates who felt no regret for asking questions.

3

Complete the chart below by following the example. For the last two rows, add new base words.

Verb	Suffix	New Noun
bio	**-logy**	*biology*
geo	**-logy**	
cardio	**-logy**	
theo	**-logy**	
techno	**-logy**	
socio	**-logy**	
zoo	**-logy**	
	-logy	
	-logy	

A. Select four words from the above chart and create a question for your partner. Remember to start your question with a question word (Who, What, Where, When, Why, How, Is, Are, Do, Did, Does, etc.). You also want to end each question with a question mark (?). Underline each vocabulary word.

1. ____________________
2. ____________________
3. ____________________
4. ____________________

3

B. Take turns asking and answering questions with your partner. Ask your instructor to give you feedback on your questions to check your English grammar.

On Your Own

What is the best class that you have had?
Describe the teacher and the subject.
Can you list three factors that made your favorite class special?

1. ____________________
2. ____________________
3. ____________________

Discussing Quotations

In your small groups, take turns reading these quotations out loud and discuss them. Do you agree with the quotation? Disagree? Why? Mark your opinion. Afterwards, pick a favorite quotation. Remember to give a reason or an example.

1. **"It is impossible for a man to learn what he thinks he already knows."**
   —Epictetus, (55-135), stoic philosopher ☐**Agree** ☐**Disagree**

2. **"Only the educated are free."**
   —Epictetus (55-135), stoic philosopher ☐**Agree** ☐**Disagree**

3. **"The wise are instructed by reason, average minds by experience, the stupid by necessity and the brute by instinct."**
   —Marcus Cicero (106-43 BC) Roman statesman ☐**Agree** ☐**Disagree**

4. **"Teach the tongue to say 'I don't know."**
   —Maimonides (1135-1204), Jewish philosopher ☐**Agree** ☐**Disagree**

5. **"Nothing in life is to feared. It is only to be undestood."**
   —Marie Curie (1867-1934), French physicist ☐**Agree** ☐**Disagree**

6. **"Education is helping the child realize his potentialities."**
—Erich Fromm (1900-1980), American psychoanalyst ☐**Agree** ☐**Disagree**

7. **"They know enough who know how to learn."**
—Henry Adams (1838-1918), American historian ☐**Agree** ☐**Disagree**

8. **"Education is a progressive discovery of our own ignorance."**
—Will Durant (1885-1981), American historian ☐**Agree** ☐**Disagree**

3

9. **"The highest result of education is tolerance."**
—Helen Keller (1880-1968), American author ☐**Agree** ☐**Disagree**

10. **"Education is a kind of continuing dialogue and a dialogue assumes, in the nature of the case, different points of view."**
—Robert Hutchins (1899-1977), American educator ☐**Agree** ☐**Disagree**

Discussion: Which was your favorite quote? Why?

____

____

____

The Conversation Continues

Billy Pham | www.billypham.com

Let's continue to explore topics related to school and knowledge with one or two classmates. Use complete sentences to respond.

3

1. Did you ever have a tutor, join a study group, or go to a cram school? Why?
2. Do you remember taking class or school field trips? Where did you go?
3. What did you enjoy most about school?
4. What kind of problems did the school have?
5. Were you often given homework? Was it too much, too little, or just right?
6. How did your teachers evaluate your work? How did your parents encourage you to study hard?
7. Did you wear a uniform to school? What did it look like?
8. Which after-school activities, clubs, or sports did you participate in?
9. What sports were popular in your school?
10. What are you proud of achieving in your academic studies?
11. What was your best school year? Why?
12. Did you find a role model or mentor (teacher, coach) at your school? Who?
13. Have you kept in touch with anyone from your high school? How?
14. How are schools different today than when you went to high school?
15. Can you compare and contrast schools in two countries?
16. How can schools do better? How can we improve schools?

Pronunciation Corner

Word Stress

While Vietnamese has five tones when saying a word, English has only two: stress and unstress. In every English word of more than one syllable, one syllable is stressed the most. The vowel sound in the stressed syllable is **longer**, **louder**, and **higher** in pitch.

Pair work: Noun vs. Verb

The following two-syllable words have a noun and verb form. When a two-syllable word can be used as either a noun or a verb, the noun form is usually stressed on the **first syllable** and the **verb** is usually stressed on the **second syllable**.

Student A: Read the word as either a noun(a) or verb(b). Choose an equal amount of nouns and verbs to practice.

Student B: Listen and underline the stressed syllables. Say if it's a noun or verb; then read aloud the matching sentence that contains the noun or verb that your partner said.

Example:

Student A: contract
Student B: Noun. He signed the **con**tract

A. conflict	He had a **con**flict with his best friend.
B. conflict	Their schedules con**flict** with mine.
A. export	The **ex**port of wine is popular.
B. export	The U.S. ex**ports** a lot of products.
A. present	Here's a **pre**sent from Sarah.
B. present	The sisters pre**sent** their talents well.
A. reject	That shirt is a **re**ject from the factory.
B. reject	Universities re**ject** many applications every year.
A. suspect	She is a murder **sus**pect.
B. suspect	The police sus**pect** him of murder.

Culture Corner

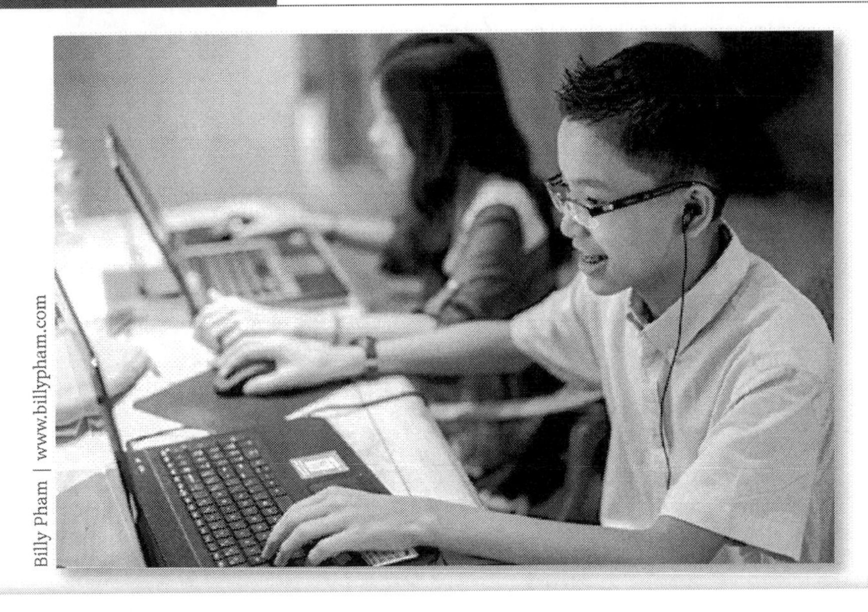
Billy Pham | www.billypham.com

From: cute_boy_2016@hothot.com
Sent: Sunday, October 22, 2016 4:49 AM
To: teacher@school.edu
Subject:

hello ,im Aladin i didnt found the home work in the library , and i want to tell you that i cant attend the class tmorrow because i have a dmv appointment

Email has become a part of our daily life in the 21st century. We send so many emails that we sometimes forget the difference between casual and more formal types of communication. As a result, emails are documents that can make positive or negative impressions. Also, it can document in print our feelings or thoughts at a particular point in time. That's one reason why investigators and lawyers often seek emails during the first stage of investigations and lawsuits. Email etiquette, therefore, is more than just good manners; it's an essential skill for modern professionals in school and the workplace.

3

What could go wrong?

Let's work together in small groups and create a list of potential mistakes that students and professionals can make in writing emails. Be prepared to share your answers with the entire class.

1. *Reveal secrets*
2. ______
3. ______
4. ______

Being Professional in College

When writing to your instructor, use your college or university email. Using your campus email shows your instructor that the email is school related and not spam. If you don't have a campus email, use a neutral email address that does not give an unprofessional, or even potentially negative impression. Your email address should be based on your real name, not a username or nickname. If you have a popular name, use periods [.], hyphens [-], or underscores [_] to help you get a unique email address.

Activity 1: Put a check next to the appropriate email addresses to use.

Name: Hào Nguyễn

______ hnguyen@ymail.com
______ krazie_guy@hotmail.com
______ haong@yahoo.com
______ kungfupanda4eva@gmail.com
______ diehard99@yahoo.com
______ nguyen_hao@gmail.com
______ youngnhot23@hotmail.com

Note

The appropriate email addresses focus on information. They may sound boring, but sometimes boring is also professional.

Always use the subject line. When filling in the subject line, make sure that it's short and clear because you don't want your email to appear like one that may end up in the spam folder. Try to include the class title, time, name and topic of email because your instructor may teach more than one class or have other students with the same name as you. You want to make your writing clear to your reader. Doesn't that make sense?

Example: ALI 245 Homework – Request for Extension
Feeling Ill and Seeing a Doctor Today
Oral Language. 10:00. Thảo – Homework

Address your instructor directly. Use an acceptable salutation to start the email such as "Dear…" or "Hello…" Following the greeting should be the person's title (Mr., Mrs., Ms., or Dr.) with their last name followed by a comma or colon. Using the last name is more formal and should be used, unless you are on a familiar first-name basis with your teacher. Remember, American teachers don't like to be called "Teacher." You should call your instructor by their name, based on their preference.

3

Too Casual	Too Formal
What you doing teacher	Most highest sir,
Hello beautiful teacher	Dear Most Esteemed Professor
Yo, teacher!	Dear Excellency
Hi Prof!	
Hi, dude!	
Yo	
Boss man,	

Greet the reader. Set a tone and greet the reader. Don't start with your request, or you may seem rude. So we first use a kind way of wishing well.

- I hope this email finds you well
- I hope all is well with you.

Second, introduce yourself if necessary by including your full name, class and meeting time. Your teacher may have a large class or your instructor may teach multiple sections of the same class.

Write the actual message. Keep your message short by focusing on the main points. Do not just go on and on and on and on and on… Your instructor has to read many emails each day so get to the point and be polite. "Please" and "thank you" should be used to show respect. Never write emails when you're angry because you want to appear professional.

Format the message into short paragraphs by topics to make your message easier to understand. Remember to insert a line space between each paragraph. You can also indent the paragraphs if you want. Last but not least, avoid very informal writing (e.g. I don't wanna miss your class but…), slang words, and emoticons.

Use a correct closing. End your email with something polite.

Activity 2: Put a check next to each of the appropriate closings to use to your teacher

______	Love,	______	Thanks,
______	Thinking of you,	______	Dreaming of you,
______	Sincerely,	______	Hugs and kisses,
______	Regards,	______	Respectfully,
______	Yours cordially,	______	Later,
______	See you in class,	______	That's all,

Sign with your full name. You can also include your major and school. Do not use emoticons. You are a serious student and a future professional. Read some common mistakes that college students make in signing their emails.

Signatures to avoid: Hào Nguyễn :)
Hào Nguyễn ^^
Hào Nguyễn (^^)"

Grammar and spellcheck. Proof read your message for spelling and grammar mistakes. If your email program doesn't provide automatic grammar and spellcheck options, you can copy and paste your message into a word processor. Revise, if necessary, and then copy and paste it back into your email.

NOTE: Don't write your email as though you're texting a friend. Make sure your message has full sentences, proper grammar, and correct spelling (not texting abbreviations). Don't write in all capital letters because it is commonly interpreted as SCREAMING. Again, act like a professional in your email exchanges with your teachers and other school officials.

Activity 3: Write a professional email to your instructor. Send it before class tomorrow.

Clara Hutzler | www.hellosuitcase.com

Search & Share

Collecting Academic Advice on the Internet

Billy Pham | www.billypham.com

Student Name:

Date:

3

Find a video online that provides tips for success in school or college. The video might suggest ways to improve test scores, get better grades, choose a college, get along with a roommate, or some other aspect of succeeding in school. Watch the video, take notes, and review the video for your classmates.

Video Title: _______ Length: _______

Web Address: _______ Creator: _______

1. Describe the video.
2. What tips did the video provide?
3. What was the most important idea? Why?
4. Where do you think the video was produced? Why?
5. How practical did you find the advice? Why?
6. What was the strongest part? Why?
7. What was the weakest part? Why?
8. Who do you think is the best audience for this video?
9. Why did you choose this video?
10. On a scale of 1–5, with 5 being the highest, how do you rate this video? Why?

> **"Education is learning what you didn't even know you didn't know."**
> —Daniel J. Boorstin (1914–2004), American historian

Being Home

> **"Where we love is home – home that our feet may leave, but not our hearts."**
> —Oliver Wendell Holmes, Sr. (1809-1894),
> American physician and author

Getting Started

Billy Pham | www.billypham.com

Directions:
Decide who will be Student A and who will be Student B. Student A stays on this page while Student B turns to the Answer Key on page **204**. Student A describes the picture below with as many details as possible. Meanwhile, Student B carefully listens and draws what was described in the empty box. Fill in the box. Few of us are artists so just do your best. Have fun. Switch. Compare your drawings for accuracy and effort.

Hint:

This activity is very hard, but quite helpful in describing places. Remember to use adjectives in the descriptions.

Student A:

4

Sharing Experiences

Everybody lives somewhere. Share the story of your home with a conversation partner by responding to these questions. Feel free to add other questions.

4

Tyler Tai Nguyen | www.hi-resmotion.com

1. What does your home look like on the outside? Inside?
2. How long have you lived there? How many people live in your home?
3. Which room is the "heart" of your current home? Kitchen? Living room? Why?
4. Where do you park your car? Motorbike? Bicycle?
5. How has your home changed since you started living there?
6. Can you talk about your neighborhood? What's it like to live there?
7. Is your home in a convenient location? Can you give an example?
8. Are there any parks nearby?
9. What do you like to do at home? What are some domestic pleasures?
10. What paintings, posters, or other artwork do you have?
11. Do you have any pets? What's their favorite spot?
12. What, if any, plants or flowers do you have? Where are they?
13. What are some chores that must be done to keep your home beautiful?
14. How many different homes have you lived in? Which did you like best? Why?
15. What are you looking for in your next home? Why?

Word List

Which words do you already know? Underline them, and circle the words you are unsure about. Then review your answers with a partner.

Noun	Verb	Adjective
appliance /ờ.plai.âns/	**lease /lís/**	**exterior /ès.stia.rì.ờ/**
checklist /chéc.lís/	***purchase /pơ.chìs/**	homesick /hôm.sík/
*fee /phi/		**interior /ìn.thia.rì.ờ/**
lease /lís/		*external /ès.stờ.nồ/
neighbor /nêi.bờ/		
neighborhood /nêi.bờ.hừt/		
residence /re.zi.đâns/		
***purchase /pơ.chìs/**		
exterior /ès.stia.rì.ờ/		
interior /ìn.thia.rì.ờ/		

*Indicates words on the Academic Word List. See p.204 for all AWL words used in this book.

Expanding Vocabulary

Look at the definitions and example sentences below. Do the definitions match what you and your partner expected in the Word List? If not, what is different?

appliance [noun]: a machine or device that performs a particular function in the office or home; an object with a special use or purpose.

> Ex: Thảo has a coffee-maker and a toaster, but they still need a TV and a few other **appliances** at home.

checklist [noun]: a written series of items arranged top to bottom or in columns, written to insure accuracy or completeness.

> Ex: Nga made a **checklist** of what she needed from the gardening store because it was far from her house.

4

exterior [adjective]: outside; opposite of interior.
[noun]: the outside of a house, room, object or area; the outer part of a place or thing.

> Ex: **Exterior** paint must be stronger than interior paint because it must protect against rain and snow.

external [adjective]: outside or something related to the outside.

> Ex: Be careful about **external** costs; we have a tight budget this year.

fee [noun]: money paid for a service; the cost to use something of value owned by someone else.

> Ex: You have to pay a small **fee** to register a new motorcycle in Hồ Chí Minh.

homesick [adjective]: feeling lonely, missing one's family or home.

> Ex: She got **homesick** for her family after two weeks away.

interior [adjective]: inside; opposite of exterior.
[noun]: the inside of a house, room, object or area; the inner part of a place or thing.

> Ex: The restaurant's **interior**, bright and bold, gave the new restaurant a modern, hip

lease [noun]: a contract made to obtain the use of something (home, business, car) for a specified price over a specified period of time; a period of time covered by a contract.
[verb]: to rent for the use of something (home, business, car) for a set period of time.

> Ex: My apartment **lease** ends next month.
> I **lease** my car for tax purposes.

neighbor [noun]: a person living next door or nearby.

> Ex: The **neighbor** feeds the cats when I leave town.

neighborhood [noun]: a particular section of a city.

> **Ex:** They liked the **neighborhood** because it had a lovely park and a good school.

purchase [verb]: to buy something.
[noun]: something that is bought.

> **Ex:** Where did you **purchase** those beautiful shoes?
> The Louisana **Purchase** more than doubled the size of the United States in 1803, and added approximately 828,000 square miles to the country.

4

residence [noun]: a place one lives; the act or fact of living in a specific place as one's home.

> **Ex:** My school **residence** is in California where I study, but my true home is back with my family in Hà Nội.

? Asking Questions with New Vocabulary Words

Tyler Tai Nguyen | www.hi-resmotion.com

A. Select five vocabulary words in this chapter and write a question for each word. Remember to start with a question word (Who, What, Where, When, Why, How, Is, Are, Do, Did, Does, etc.). You also want to end each question with a question mark (?). Underline each vocabulary word.

Example: *Is this a new appliance?*

1. ____________________
2. ____________________
3. ____________________
4. ____________________
5. ____________________

B. Take turns asking and answering questions with your partner or group members. Ask your instructor to give you feedback your English grammar.

Paraphrasing Proverbs

4

Read the following proverbs and discuss them with your partner. Write what you think they mean in the spaces provided. Circle your favorites. Explain your choices.

Vietnamese:

Neighbors are better than distant relatives.
"Bà con xa không bằng láng giềng gần"
Meaning:____________________________________

Rivers have sections, people have times.
"Sông có khúc người có lúc."
Meaning:____________________________________

Near black ink — dark, near light — bright.
"Gần mực thì đen, gần đèn thì sáng."
Meaning:____________________________________

International:

Home is where the heart is. —English
Meaning:____________________________________

Birds return to old nests. —Japanese
Meaning:____________________________________

A house is not a home. —American
Meaning:____________________________________

Anger in a home is like rottenness in a fruit. —Hebrew
Meaning:____________________________________

Building Words

The Latin Prefix "ex-"

Prefix	Meaning	Example
ex-	out	The words claim, exclaim, and proclaim are closely related. Claim is to say something, "**ex**claim" to push out the words with excitement, and proclaim to publicly say something before a large crowd.
ex-	outside	A beautiful "**ex**terior" improves the value of a house, and a beautiful interior turns a house into a home.

The common prefix "ex" meaning out/outside comes from Latin. We see this prefix in many daily situations.

Complete the chart below by following the example. For the last two rows, add new roots and create new words.

Prefix	Base	New Word
ex-	terior	*exterior*
ex-	change	
ex-	claim	
ex-	clude	
ex-	hibit	
ex-	hale	
ex-	plore	
ex-	plicit	
ex-	pose	
ex-	press	
ex-		
ex-		

Note: We also sometimes use the prefix "ex" in hyphenated words to mean the old or previous person in a position. Some examples include: ex-classmate, ex-president, ex-boss, ex-roommate.

A. Select four words from the above chart and create a question for your partner. Remember to start your question with a question word (Who, What, Where, When, Why, How, Is, Are, Do, Did, Does, etc.). You also want to end each question with a question mark (?). Underline each vocabulary word.

1. ______________________________
2. ______________________________
3. ______________________________
4. ______________________________

4

B. Take turns asking and answering questions with your partner. Ask your instructor to give you feedback on your questions to check your English grammar.

Discussing Quotations

In your small groups, take turns reading these quotations out loud and discuss them. Do you agree with the quotation? Disagree? Why? Mark your opinion. Afterwards, pick a favorite quotation. Remember to give a reason or an example.

1. **"He is happiest, be he king or peasant, who finds peace in his home."**
   —Johann Wolfgang von Goethe (1749–1832), German writer ☐**Agree** ☐**Disagree**

2. **"A man's home is his castle."**
   —Sir Edward Coke (1552–1634), English lord/statesman ☐**Agree** ☐**Disagree**

3. **"Home: The place where when you have to go there, they have to take you in."**
   —Robert Frost (1875–1963), American poet ☐**Agree** ☐**Disagree**

4. **"A house is not a home unless it contains food and fire for the mind as well as the body."**
   —Benjamin Franklin (1706-1790), American statesman ☐**Agree** ☐**Disagree**

5. **"Determine what sort of a house will be fit for you; determine to work for it, and to get one that you can entirely enjoy and manage."**
   —John Ruskin (1819-1900), English critic ☐**Agree** ☐**Disagree**

6. **"No matter under what circumstances you leave it, home does not cease to be home. No matter how you lived there—well or poorly."**
—Joseph Brodsky (1940–1996), Russian-American/poet, Nobel Prize winner (1987)
☐ **Agree** ☐ **Disagree**

7. **"Home is the girl's prison and the woman's workhouse."**
—George Bernard Shaw (1856–1950), Irish writer, Nobel Prize winner (1925)
☐ **Agree** ☐ **Disagree**

8. **"The best way to keep children at home is make the home atmosphere pleasant, and let the air out of the tires."**
—Dorothy Parker (1893–1967), American writer
☐ **Agree** ☐ **Disagree**

9. **"Modern apartments are built on the principle that half as much room should cost twice as much money."**
—Evan Esar (1899–1995), American humorist
☐ **Agree** ☐ **Disagree**

10. **"Have nothing in your house that you do not know to be useful, or believe to be beautiful."**
—William Morris (1834-1896), English artist/writer
☐ **Agree** ☐ **Disagree**

Discussion: Which was your favorite quote? Why?

___

___

___

The Conversation Continues

Let's continue to explore topics related to the home with one or two classmates. Use complete sentences to respond.

Tyler Tai Nguyen | www.hi-resmotion.com

4

1. If you could change one thing about your current home, what would it be?
2. What is in your bedroom?
3. Which room do you spend the most time in? Least time in? Why?
4. What are some things in your home that you can't live without?
5. Have you ever felt homesick? When?
6. What makes a good neighbor? Why?
7. Is your old neighborhood the same today as it was when you were a child?
8. Would you rather live in an apartment or a house? Why?
9. Would you rather live in a city or the countryside? Why?
10. Where is a good place to find interior design ideas?
11. Describe your dream house. What modern appliances would your dream house have?
12. Do you see real estate as a good investment? Why?
13. Would you rather invest money in a house or keep it in the bank? Why?
14. What makes a house a home for you?
15. What do you think houses in the future will be like?

On Your Own

Select five adjectives (e.g. spacious, cozy) for your dream home:

1. ______________________
2. ______________________
3. ______________________

Let's expand your dream. Use the worksheet "My Dream Home" at the end of this chapter

Pronunciation Corner

Word Stress

In English, shifts between voiced and voiceless consonants are required to tell the difference between specific words. These features do not exist in Vietnamese; thus, it often causes problems for Vietnamese learners.

A voiced consonant is a consonant that uses your voice. To test, place your hand on your throat. If you feel a vibration, then the consonant is voiced. If you do not feel a vibration then the consonant is voiceless. Note: When you are whispering, you are not voicing any sounds.

Row by row, practice saying each sound, switching back and forth until you can hear the difference between the voiced and voiceless consonant sounds.

voiced	voiceless
/b/ [bear]	/p/ [pear]
/z/ [zip]	/s/ [sip]
/d/ [door]	/t/ [tore]
/g/ [gate]	/k/ or /c/ [Kate]
/j/ [Jane]	/ch/ [chain]
/v/ [leave]	/f/ [leaf]

4

Pair work: Which word is different? /s/ and /z/

Student A: Read the words in Part A.
Student B: Listen and mark the column for the word that is different in Part B.

Switch but do not say the words in the same order.

Part A:

	A	B	C
1.	**s**ip	**s**ip	**z**ip
2.	fu**ss**	fu**zz**	fu**ss**
3.	bu**s**ing	bu**s**ing	bu**zz**ing
4.	rai**s**ing	ra**c**ing	ra**c**ing
5.	**z**oo	**s**ue	**s**ue
6.	play**s**	pla**ce**	pla**ce**
7.	**z**eal	**s**eal	**s**eal
8.	bu**s**	bu**s**	bu**zz**

Part B:

	A	B	C
1.			
2.			
3.			
4.			
5.			
6.			
7.			
8.			

Culture Corner

4

Personal Space

Photographer | Tung Phan

How close is too close? Personal space is the invisible amount of physical space considered culturally appropriate between yourself and others when meeting and talking.

Americans tend to require more "elbow room" than other cultures. They usually appreciate a bit more distance around them. If you stand too close to an American during your conversation, they might feel that you are "in their face;" many Americans will automatically pull back to restore a more comfortable distance.

Public Setting 12 ft. or more (3.6 m.)

Clara Hutzler | www.hellosuitcase.com

Public settings may be reserved for public events and formal speeches. At events such as concerts, assemblies, worship services, graduations, and similar communal events, the greater the status of the guest, the larger the distance from the audience so that all attendees are included. A priest or minister, for example, might speak from behind a podium on a stage in a house of worship and reflection such as a church, temple, or synagogue.

Social Setting 4ft. (1.2 m.)

Clara Hutzler | www.hellosuitcase.com

We often meet acquaintances and strangers in social settings such as parties and museums. The distance and comfort level in social settings vary. In the beginning, it is safer to keep more of a distance. As you continue to speak with the individual, a closer distance may feel comfortable. The easiest way to handle this: when you first meet someone, say your greeting, shake hands, and step back a bit.

Personal Setting 1.5 ft. (0.45 m.)

Billy Pham | www.billypham.com

Personal settings are reserved for conversations with family and close friends that you've come to trust and treasure.

4

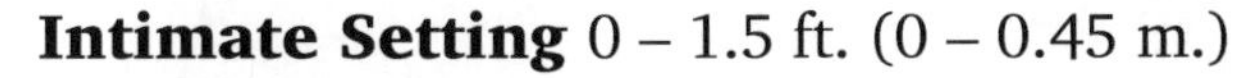

Intimate Setting 0 – 1.5 ft. (0 – 0.45 m.)

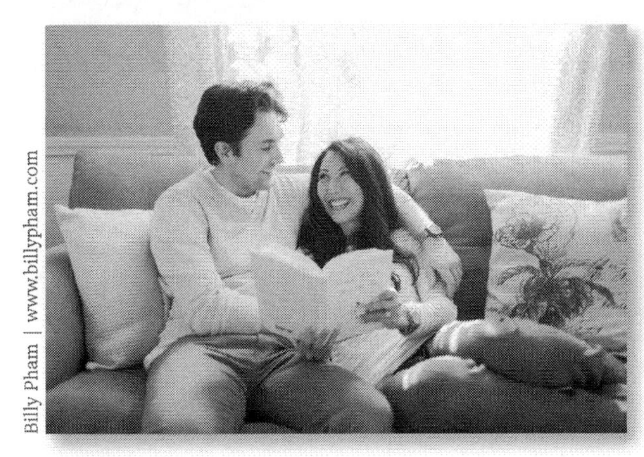

Billy Pham | www.billypham.com

Closer, more private settings between close friends, lovers, and family can be called intimate space. When entering such an intimate space, permission is needed or else it could be perceived as a threat. In situations like a crowded elevator or subway, where close physical contact is unavoidable, keep it impersonal by avoiding eye contact and keeping your hands to yourself.

Activity 1: With a partner, discuss the differences and similarities of personal space in the United States and another country you've lived in or visited.

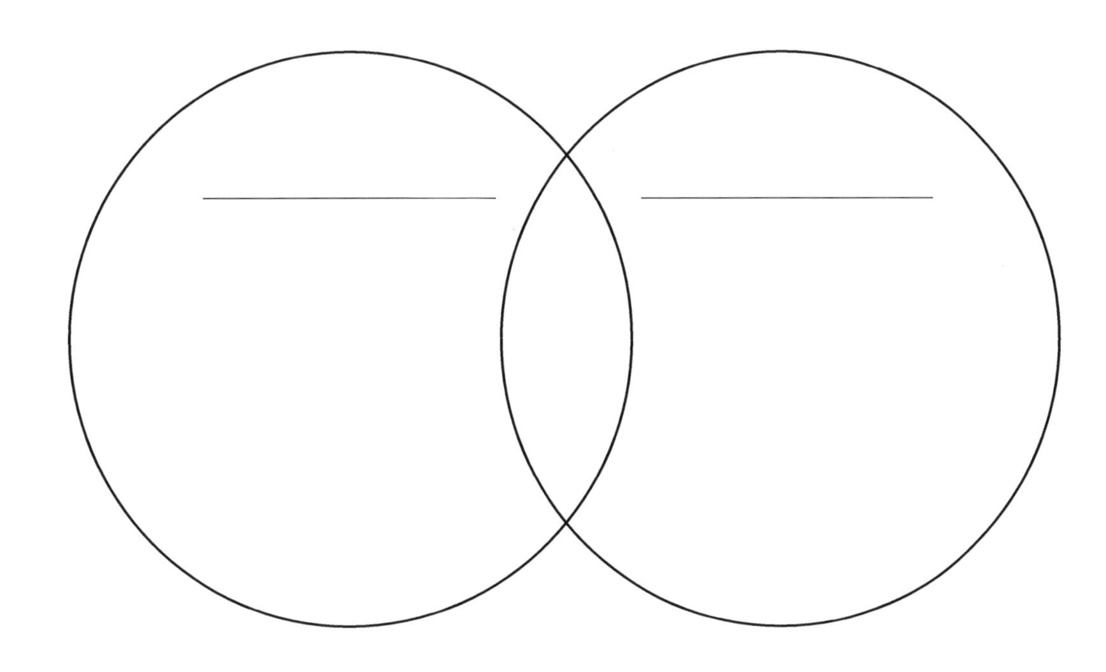

Search & Share

Airbnb: My Dream Home

Student Name:_______________ Date:_______________

4

Tyler Tai Nguyen | www.hi-resmotion.com

What is your dream home? First, go to **www.airbnb.com** and choose your dream destination. Second, search for your dream home. How many bedrooms? How many bathrooms? Does it have a view? Now describe the dream home that you would like to live in. Use the vocabulary you learned in this lesson. Use your imagination. Dream big!

Destination: _______________

1. What does the outside of your dream home look like?
2. How would you describe the neighborhood?
3. How many rooms are there?
4. Describe the kitchen:
5. Describe the living room:
6. Describe another room:
7. What else makes this home special?
8. What other information or details can you share?
9. Who will live with you in your dream home?

> **"There is a role and function for beauty in our time."**
> —Tadao Ando (1941-), Japanese architect

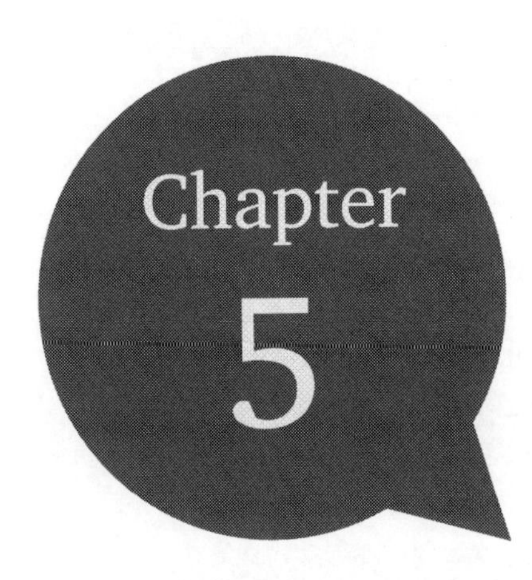

Family Bonds

"Tennis is just a game; family is forever."
— Serena Williams (1981-), American professional tennis player

Photographer | Tung Phan

Getting Started

What do you know about my family?

Directions:
Write three statements about your family below. Two of the statements must be true and one must be a lie. Do not show what you've written to anyone. Read your statements to your partner or classmates in no particular order. Allow your classmate(s) to ask you questions about each statement before guessing which one is the lie.

5

Photographer | Tung Phan

Truth:

Truth:

Lie:

Sharing Experiences

Family remains the center of society. Share your experiences and discover your partner's many experiences as a family member.

Billy Pham | www.billypham.com

1. Do you have a large, medium, or small family? How many people are in your family?
2. What are your parents' names? How do you spell their names?
3. Where were your parents born? Were they born in a hospital?
4. How did your parents meet? What attracted them to each other?
5. How many siblings do you have? Are you the oldest? Youngest?
6. What do you enjoy doing with your siblings?
7. Why do you think siblings sometimes fight?
8. When does the extended family with multiple generations usually get together? Does your family have reunions?
9. Do you live with your nuclear family or your extended family? How many generations live in your home now?
10. Does your extended family have a leader or dominant figure? Is there a patriarch or a matriarch?
11. How can family members support and help each other?
12. Do you have a favorite aunt, uncle, or cousin? Why?
13. What language or languages did you hear in your childhood home?
14. Which languages are spoken in home now?
15. Do you exchange gifts on holidays? Which holidays?
16. What do you appreciate about your family?

Word List

Which words do you already know? Underline them, and circle the words you are unsure about. Then review your answers with a partner.

Noun	Verb	Adjective
ancestor /an.sés.tờ/		
extended family /ès.ten.địt/ /pham.mờ.lì/		
half-brother /háph.bra.đờ/		
in-law /in.lo/		
matriarch /mây.trì.ọk/		
nuclear family /nu.kly.ờ/		
patriarch /pây.trì.ọk/		
reunion /rì.du.nhần/		
spouse /sbaos/		
step-sister /stéb.sís.tờ/		
*generation /jen.nờ.rây.shần/		
*hierarchy /hai.ơ.óc.kỳ/		

*Indicates words on the Academic Word List. See p.204 for all AWL words used in this book.

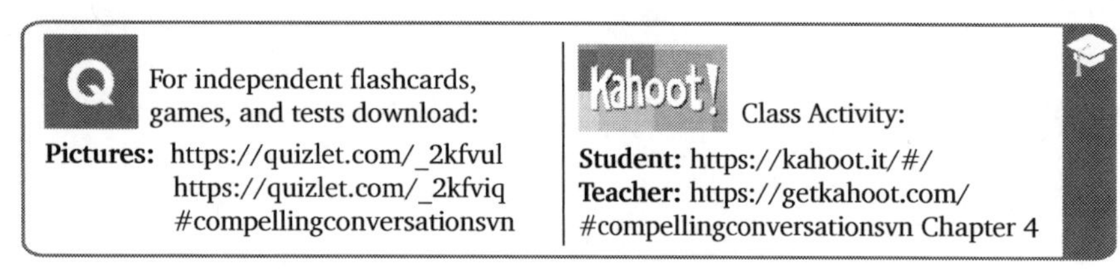

Expanding Vocabulary

Look at the definitions and example sentences below. Do the definitions match what you and your partner expected in the Word List? If not, what is different?

ancestor [noun]: an early member of the family, clan, or tribe.

> **Ex:** My **ancestors** came from Bình Dương.

extended family [noun]: a large family with aunts, uncles, cousins, grandparents.

> **Ex:** Our **extended families** attended the huge wedding party in Huế.

5

generation [noun]: all the people born from a set of parents within a family; all the people of about the same age in a society.

> **Ex:** My **generation** is smaller than my father's generation, but we will still have a big family wedding with four generations celebrating together next June.

half-brother [noun]: a male sibling who has just one parent in common with other siblings.

> **Ex:** Phương was my **half-brother**; we shared the same mother, but had different fathers.

hierarchy [noun]: a system of ranking people, often by status or power.

> **Ex:** What's the **hierarchy** here? Who makes the decisions?

in-law [noun]: member of the family through marriage; a relative due to marriage.

> **Ex:** I love my mother-**in-law** and respect my father-in-law.

matriarch [noun]: the female head of a family.

> **Ex:** My grandmother is the **matriarch** of our family and hosts our family gatherings.

nuclear family [noun]: a single family group: a family unit of only parents and children.

> **Ex:** A typical American **nuclear family** might be a father, mother, and two children.

patriarch [noun]: the male head of a family.

> **Ex:** A **patriarch** makes many family decisions and is respected.

reunion [noun]: a gathering of people in a common group that have often not seen each other for a long time.

> **Ex:** Family **reunions** are more popular than college reunions.

spouse [noun]: a wife or husband.

> **Ex:** My husband is my **spouse**, my best friend, and the father of my children.

stepsister [noun]: the daughter of one's stepmother or stepfather.

> **Ex:** My **stepsister** and I became good friends.

5

Asking Questions with New Vocabulary Words

A. Select five vocabulary words in this chapter and write a question for each word. Remember to start your question with a question word (Who, What, Where, When, Why, How, Is, Are, Do, Did, Does, etc.). End each question with a question mark (?). Underline each vocabulary word.

Example: *Do many extended families live in your city?*

1. ______________________
2. ______________________
3. ______________________
4. ______________________
5. ______________________

B. Take turns asking and answering questions with your partner or group members. Ask your instructor to give you feedback on your English grammar.

Remember

- Listen carefully
- Speak carefully
- Skip awkward

Paraphrasing Proverbs

Read the following proverbs and discuss them with your partner. Write what you think they mean in the spaces provided. Circle your favorites. Explain your choices.

Vietnamese:

Brothers are like hands and feet. Brothers that get along are two happy bodies.
"Anh em như thể tay chân. Anh em hòa thuận hai thân vui vầy."
Meaning: ______________________

Brothers should get along. Others will laugh if you have differences.
"Anh em ăn ở thuận hòa. Chớ điều chếch lệch người ta chê cười."
Meaning:____

Bitterness is still family. Sweetness is still outsiders.
"Đắng cay cũng thể ruột rà, ngọt ngào cho lắm cũng là người dưng."
Meaning:____

International:

Half of your fortune lies in your family line. —Korean
Meaning:____

5

Of all the virtues, family duty is the first. —Chinese
Meaning:____

A brother helped by a brother is like a fortified city. —Latin
Meaning:____

Like father, like son. —Latin
Meaning:____

Whoever marries for money will have unworthy children. —Russian
Meaning:____

Building Words

Using the Latin Suffix "-ment"

How do we turn verbs into nouns? One method is adding a Latin suffix such as "ment" that shows an action or resulting state. The verb "agree" becomes the noun "agreement" because it is the result of people agreeing. We make many kinds of formal agreements (documents) and informal agreements (unwritten) in our lives.

Suffix	Meaning	Example
-ment	action	The "argu**ment**" went on for too long, and suddenly nobody felt comfortable.
-ment	resulting state	The guests enjoyed the meal, and the host appreciated the guest's "enjoy**ment**" of her delicious food.

5

Complete the chart below by following the example. For the last two rows, add new root words.

Prefix	Base	New Word
agree	**-ment**	*agreement*
argue	**-ment**	
commit	**-ment**	
*comply	**-ment**	
disagree	**-ment**	
enforce	**-ment**	
enjoy	**-ment**	
displace	**-ment**	
govern	**-ment**	
invest	**-ment**	
amend	**-ment**	
adjust	**-ment**	
entertain	**-ment**	
equip	**-ment**	
	-ment	
	-ment	

A. Select four words from the above chart and create a question for your partner. Remember to start your question with a question word (Who, What, Where, When, Why, How, Is, Are, Do, Did, Does, etc.). You also want to end each question with a question mark (?). Underline each vocabulary word.

1. ____
2. ____
3. ____
4. ____

B. Take turns asking and answering questions with your partner. Ask your instructor to give you feedback on your questions to check your English grammar.

5

Discussing Quotations

In your small groups, take turns reading these quotations out loud and discuss them. Do you agree with the quotation? Disagree? Why? Mark your opinion. Afterwards, pick a favorite quotation. Remember to give a reason or an example.

1. **"All happy families resemble one another; every unhappy family is unhappy in its own fashion."**
   —Leo Tolstoy (1828–1910), Russian novelist ☐ **Agree** ☐ **Disagree**

2. **"We never know the love of a parent until we become parents ourselves."**
   —Henry Ward Beecher (1813–1887), American speaker ☐ **Agree** ☐ **Disagree**

3. **"Rearing a family is probably the most difficult job in the world."**
   —Virginia Satir (1916–1988), American therapist ☐ **Agree** ☐ **Disagree**

4. **"There are fathers who do not love their children; there is no grandfather who does not adore his grandson."**
   —Victor Hugo (1802-1885), French novelist ☐ **Agree** ☐ **Disagree**

5. **"Everyone needs to have access both to grandparents and grandchildren in order to be a full human being."**
   —Margaret Mead (1901-1978), American anthropologist ☐ **Agree** ☐ **Disagree**

6. **"We must learn to live together as brothers or perish as fools."**
   —Dr. Martin Luther King, Jr. (1929–1968), American leader, Nobel Prize winner (1964) ☐ **Agree** ☐ **Disagree**

7. **"When you are a mother, you're never really alone in your thoughts. A mother always has to think twice, once for herself and once for her child."**
—Sophia Loren (1934–), Italian actress ☐ **Agree** ☐ **Disagree**

8. **"There can be no situation in life in which the conversation of my dear sister will not administer some comfort to me."**
—Mary Montagu (1689-1762), English writer ☐ **Agree** ☐ **Disagree**

9. **"A sister can be seen as someone who is both ourselves and very much not ourselves, a special kind of double."**
—Toni Morrison (1931-), American novelist/Nobel Prize winner (1993) ☐ **Agree** ☐ **Disagree**

10. **"In every conceivable manner, the family is the link to our past, and the bridge to our future."**
—Alex Haley (1921-1992), American author ☐ **Agree** ☐ **Disagree**

Discussion: Which was your favorite quote? Why?

____

____

____

The Conversation Continues

Let's continue to explore topics related to family with one or two classmates. Use complete sentences to respond.

Clara Hutzler | www.hellosuitcase.com

1. What days were special for your family when you were a child?
2. Which relative do you feel closest to? Why? What makes that relationship special?

3. Do you resemble anyone in your family? In what ways?
4. How do you keep in touch with distant relatives?
5. What were some important events in your family history?
6. Which ancestor would you most like to meet? Why?
7. Why do you think divorce has become so common in the United States?
8. What might cause someone to become a "black sheep" in a family?
9. How do family habits and traditions differ in the U.S. than in Vietnam?
10. How can families create stress? How can families provide comfort?
11. How can people build stronger and healthier family relationships?
12. Are relative or friends more important? Why?
13. What are some of your favorite childhood memories with your family?
14. What's the most important thing your parents taught you?
15. If you could have a different number of siblings, what would it be? Why?

Pronunciation Corner

Voiced /v/ vs. Voiceless /f/

In the previous chapter, we learned the importance of voiced and voiceless consonants, specifically /s/ and /z/. In this chapter we will focus on /v/ and /f/. To make both sounds, the upper teeth touch the back of the lower lip. Remember that the position is the same but the sounds are different: /v/ voiced and /f/ voiceless.

Pair work: Which word is different? /v/ and /f/

Student A: Read the words.

	A	B	C
1.	half	half	have
2.	save	safe	safe
3.	fat	vat	fat
4.	fine	fine	vine
5.	vault	fault	fault
6.	service	surface	service
7.	prove	proof	proof
8.	believe	belief	believe
9.	ferry	very	very

Student B: Listen and mark the column for the word that is different.

	A	B	C
1.			
2.			
3.			
4.			
5.			
6.			
7.			
8.			
9.			

Culture Corner

Titles

Using the correct title when first meeting someone is important in contemporary society. If the other person is clearly older than you or you are meeting them for the first time, use a title and the last name. Please keep in mind that Americans use a title followed by the last name only.

Example: Mr. Smith, not Mr. John
Example: Dr. Pham, not Dr. Thuy Pham

Titles Defined

- Mr. + last name = Used to address men

Pronounced as /mis.stờ/

- Mrs. + last name = Used to address married women

Pronounced as /mis.sis/

- Miss + last name = Used to address unmarried or single women

Pronounced as /mis/

- Ms. + last name = Used to address both married and unmarried women. It is con sidered the "Mr." equivalent because it doesn't declare the marital status.

Pronounced as /miz/

If the other person has a title such as "Doctor" or "Dean," use that title and the last name instead of the above titles.

Note: Many professors and other professionals have worked many years to earn their titles, and expect public recognition of their hard work and achievement. Therefore, some professors insist on students addressing them as "Dr. Meyers" or "Dr. Lee." These professors are real doctors – even if they do not work in hospitals like medical doctors who physically treat patients and save lives.

Activity:

Your American friend, Jenny Robinson, invites you over for dinner with her family. With a partner, discuss how you would greet each person. Make sure to use the appropriate title for each person.

Billy Pham | www.billypham.com

Classroom Activity: Role-play

Family Tree

Step 1: List your family members including your parents, grandparents, siblings, uncles, aunts, cousins, and/or children. Give birth dates if they are known and death dates if a person is deceased.

5

Step 2: Create a family tree. Fill in the appropriate boxes with your family members. Feel free to add/delete branches as needed.

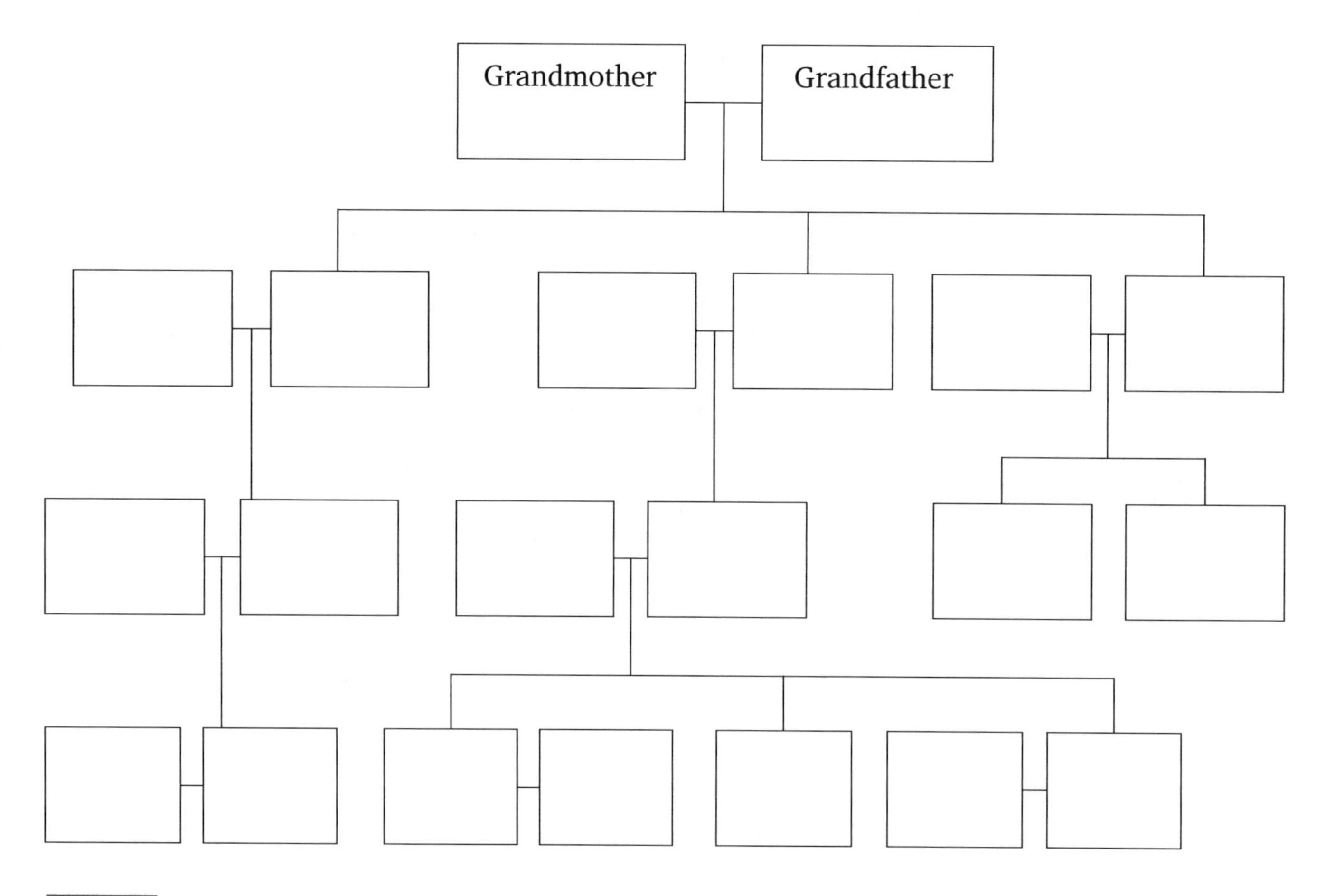

Step 3: Share your family tree with your classmates.

Search & Share

Exploring New Holidays

Student Name: ____________________

Date: ____________________

Search on the Internet for an article (in English) about a favorite holiday or celebration. Choose a holiday that you do not currently celebrate, but that you would like to know more about. Find an article, read it, print it, and discuss it with classmates.

5

Title: ____________________ Publication/Website: ____________________

Author: ____________________ Publication Date: ____________________

1. Describe the video.
2. What tips did the video provide?
3. What was the most important idea? Why?
4. Where do you think the video was produced? Why?
5. How practical did you find the advice? Why?
6. What was the strongest part? Why?
7. What was the weakest part? Why?
8. Who do you think is the best audience for this video?
9. Why did you choose this video?
10. On a scale of 1–5, with 5 being the highest, how do you rate this video? Why?

> **"Education is learning what you didn't even know you didn't know."**
> —Daniel J. Boorstin (1914–2004), American historian

Chapter 6

Delicious Choices

"Food is our common ground, a universal experience."
—James Beard (1902-1985), American author and culinary expert

Jason Q. Tran | www.jasonqtran.com

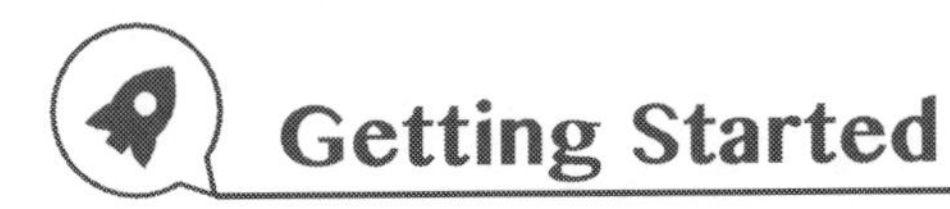

Getting Started

Name that food!

Directions:
Draw a food item in the boxes below. Do not show anyone. The purpose of this activity is for others to ask you yes/no questions in order to find out what that food item is. You can only respond to questions with "yes" or "no." Take turns asking yes/no questions until someone correctly guesses the food in the box. Remember, your classmate only has 10 questions to guess correctly what that food item is.

Photographer | Tung Phan

Sharing Experiences

Jason Q. Tran | www.jasonqtran.com

Everybody eats. Food is both a necessity and a pleasure; it remains a safe and interesting way to learn more about people and cultures. Interview your partner and share your eating and drinking experiences.

6

1. Do you consider eating a chore, a duty, or a pleasure? Why?
2. What did you eat yesterday? Was it a typical day?
3. Do you drink tea or coffee in the morning? Regular or decaffeinated?
4. Do you eat at the same time each day? Or do you eat when you have time?
5. Do you prefer salty snacks or sweet snacks? How often do you snack?
6. Where do you usually shop for food? What shopping tips can you share?
7. Which drinks do you usually have with your evening meal?
8. What kind of meat do you enjoy eating? Beef? Pork? Chicken?
9. Do you have a favorite vegetable? Are you a vegetarian?
10. What is your favorite fruit? Which fruits do you find delicious?
11. Can you name three dishes that you really enjoy or savor?
12. Which regional foods in Vietnam do you like the most?
13. What are some unique Vietnamese dishes?
14. What dishes, ingredients, or spices do you look for on menus?
15. Which Vietnamese dishes would you recommend to an American? Why?

On Your Own

Write menu descriptions for your perfect meal. Include the major ingredients of dishes that one finds on a menu. Be sure to include appetizers, beverages, and desserts. Indulge yourself. Now describe your delicious choices to your group. Be creative!

Word List

Which words do you already know? Underline them, and circle the words you are unsure about. Then review your answers with a partner.

Noun	Verb	Adjective	Adverb
chef /shéph/	savor /xê.vờ/	decaffeinated /đi.khăf.phờ.nê.địd/	fast /phas/
***label /lê.bồ/**	**feast /phís/**	edible /e.đi.bồ/	
feast /phís/	***label /lê.bồ/**	culinary /kho.lê.ne.rì/	
glutton /glất.thần/		*ethnic /éth.nịk/	
vegetarian /ve.jầ.the.rì.ần/		*available /ầ.veo.la. bồ/	

6

*Indicates words on the Academic Word List. See p.204 for all AWL words used in this book.

Expanding Vocabulary

Look at the definitions and example sentences below. Do the definitions match what you and your partner expected in the Word List? If not, what is different?

available [adjective]: ready for use on hand.

> **Ex:** What fruits are **available** this time of year?

chef [noun]: a professional cook; the head cook in a restaurant.

> **Ex:** The **chef**'s specialty is a tasty seafood stew with broiled fish.

culinary [adjective]: having to do with cooking and food; related to preparation of food.

> **Ex:** Study the **culinary** arts if you want to become a chef.

decaffeinated [adjective]: containing no caffeine; a drink with the caffeine removed.

> Ex: Mỹ Dung drank **decaffeinated** coffee because regular coffee made her feel nervous and act jumpy.

edible [adjective]: something that can be eaten.

> Ex: **Edible** can be a flexible concept, often depending on how hungry you feel.

ethnic [adjective]: something relating to a group of people sharing a distinctive culture.

> Ex: Los Angeles has so many wonderful **ethnic** restaurants since people come from all over the globe to live in southern California.

fast [adverb]: moving with speed, advancing or progressing rapidly.
[noun]: a period of time without eating; verb: to go without eating.

6

> Ex: Hải Dương's motorbike can go very **fast**, but it sometimes goes slowly in city traffic.
> The word "breakfast" literally means to break the **fast**.
> Some people **fast** on holidays, and some people fast to lose weight.

feast [noun]: a large, excellent meal; an abundant amount of well-prepared food.

> Ex: My mother prepared a **feast** to celebrate my graduation.

gluttony [noun]: an excess of eating or drinking; greedy or excessive indulgence.

> Ex: **Gluttony** is a common problem among overweight Americans.

label [noun]: a tag or sticker that identifies contents inside.
[verb]: to describe or classify objects or people.

> Ex: Do you read food **labels** before buying food in the supermarket?
> We carefully **label** packages for shipment, and we double-check the labels.

savor [verb]: to really enjoy; to experience satisfaction and pleasure in taste or smell.

> Ex: Eat slowly to **savor** this delicious dinner that my grandmother prepared.

vegetarian [noun]: one who eats no meat; a meat-free diet.

> Ex: As a **vegetarian**, Bảo Hà doesn't eat meat.

Asking Questions with New Vocabulary Words

A. Select five vocabulary words in this chapter and write a question for each word. Remember to start your question with a question word (Who, What, Where, When, Why, How, Is, Are, Do, Did, Does, etc.). End each question with a question mark (?). Underline each vocabulary word.

Example: *Do you know the restaurant's chef?*

1. ______________________________
2. ______________________________
3. ______________________________
4. ______________________________
5. ______________________________

B. Take turns asking and answering questions with your partner or group members. Ask your instructor to give you feedback on your English grammar.

6

Paraphrasing Proverbs

Read the following proverbs and discuss them with your partner. Write what you think they mean in the spaces provided. Circle your favorites. Explain your choices.

Vietnamese:

Eat slow, chew carefully, full for a long time. Eat fast, hungry quickly, and stomach pain.
"Ăn chậm, nhai kỹ, no lâu. Ăn nhanh, chóng đói, lại đau dạ dày."
Meaning: ______________________________

When eating a fruit, remember the person that grew the fruit.
"Ăn quả nhớ kẻ trồng cây."
Meaning: ______________________________

Able to eat and sleep is heavenly. Not able to eat and sleep is money thrown away.
"Ăn được ngủ được là tiên. Ăn ngủ không được là tiền vứt đi."
Meaning: ______________________________

International:

Half of your fortune lies in your family line. —Korean
Meaning: ___

Of all the virtues, family duty is the first. —Chinese
Meaning: ___

A brother helped by a brother is like a fortified city. —Latin
Meaning: ___

Like father, like son. —Latin
Meaning: ___

6

Whoever marries for money will have unworthy children. —Russian
Meaning: ___

On Your Own

Culture Corner: Fun with Puns

Puns are word jokes, and English has many puns. Understanding puns can be difficult for many English language learners because some words have multiple meanings and some sounds have multiple spellings with different meanings. Understanding puns requires listeners to think like a word detective, but puns can be fun. Here are three about food:

- I'm on a seafood diet. I see food and I eat it.
- A boiled egg in the morning is hard to beat
- A hungry clock will go back for seconds.

Can you find another pun about food in English or Vietnamese?

Building Words

Using the Latin Prefix "de-"

The Latin prefix "de" usually means "removal from," and we can find many academic and common words that use this prefix. Some adults like to drink "decaf," or decaffeinated coffee. That means caffeine has been removed from the popular drink. Scholars may also "debunk" a theory meaning they removed "bunk" or "junk" by disproving a false idea with evidence.

Prefix	Meaning	Example
de-	removal of, departure from	I like "**de**caf" coffee, but I used to only drink regular coffee in the morning to help me wake up.

Complete the chart below by following the example. For the last two rows, add new base words.

Prefix	Base	New Word
de-	caffeinated	decaffeinated
de-	bunk	
de-	cipher	
de-	form	
de-	lineate	
de-	mote	
de-	nounce	
de-	press	
de-	volve	
de-		
de-		

A. Select four words from the above chart and create a question for your partner. Remember to start your question with a question word (Who, What, Where, When, Why, How, Is, Are, Do, Did, Does, etc.). You also want to end each question with a question mark (?). Underline each vocabulary word.

1. ______________________________
2. ______________________________
3. ______________________________
4. ______________________________

B. Take turns asking and answering questions with your partner. Ask your instructor to give you feedback on your questions to check your English grammar.

Discussing Quotations

In your small groups, take turns reading these quotations out loud and discuss them. Do you agree with the quotation? Disagree? Why? Mark your opinion. Afterwards, pick a favorite quotation. Remember to give a reason or an example.

1. **"Better beans and bacon in peace than cakes and ale in fear."**
   —Aesop (around 550 B.C.), Greek storyteller ☐**Agree** ☐**Disagree**

2. **"The satiated man and the hungry one do not see the same thing when they look upon a loaf of bread."**
   —Rumi (1207–1273), Persian poet and mystic ☐**Agree** ☐**Disagree**

6

3. **"If it's beautifully arranged on the plate, you know someone's fingers have been all over it."**
   —Julia Child (1912–2004), American chef/author ☐**Agree** ☐**Disagree**

4. **"Live. Love. Eat."**
   —Wolfgang Puck (1949–), American chef ☐**Agree** ☐**Disagree**

5. **"When I drink, I think; and when I think, I drink."**
   —Francois Rabelais (1495–1553), French satirist ☐**Agree** ☐**Disagree**

6. **"Edible (adj). Good to eat and wholesome to digest, as a worm to a toad, a toad to a snake, a snake to a pig, a pig to a man, and a man to a worm."**
   —Ambrose Bierce (1842–1916), American writer ☐**Agree** ☐**Disagree**

7. **"The secret of staying young is to live honestly, eat slowly, and lie about your age."**
   —Lucille Ball (1911–1989), American TV star/executive ☐**Agree** ☐**Disagree**

8. **"People who drink to drown their sorrow should be told that sorrow knows how to swim."**
   —Ann Landers (1918–2002), American advice columnist ☐**Agree** ☐**Disagree**

9. **"I thought, I called, I planned, I shopped, I schlepped, I cleaned, I chopped, I soaked, I peeled, I rinsed, I grated, I minced, I simmered, I larded, I mixed, I fried, I boiled, I baked, I sauteed, I souffleed, I flame broiled, and I sweated. So, tell me it's great!"**
   —Slogan on a novelty kitchen apron in the U.S. ☐**Agree** ☐**Disagree**

10. "More die in the United States of too much food than of too little."
—John Kenneth Galbraith (1908–2006) American economist

☐ **Agree** ☐ **Disagree**

Discussion: Which was your favorite quote? Why?

___

___

___

The Conversation Continues

6

Let's continue to explore topics related to family with one or two classmates. Use complete sentences to respond.

Jason Q. Tran | www.jasonqtran.com

1. What is your favorite restaurant? Why?
2. How often do you eat at home? In a restaurant? Why?
3. What is a typical lunch in Vietnam? What is a typical lunch in the U.S.?
4. How often does your family eat an evening meal together? Who cooks?
5. In Vietnamese culture, what foods or drinks are traditionally associated with holidays? Weddings? Birthdays? Funerals?

6. Have you ever fasted? Why? Were you hungry after skipping two meals?
7. Why do some people read food labels? Do you have any food allergies?
8. Do you cook? Do you save recipes? Can you share a favorite family recipe?
9. What is something that you eat or drink every day?
10. Can you name some restaurants in this area that serve food from other countries? What kinds of food do they serve? What's your favorite?
11. How have people's eating habits changed over the years?
12. What do you care most about in a restaurant: food, atmosphere, or customer service?
13. Have you ever had a bad restaurant experience? What happened?
14. Do you think buffets are a good value?
15. What is your favorite Vietnamese dessert? Western dessert?

Pronunciation Corner

Voiced [verbs] vs. Voiceless [nouns]

Let's return to the topic of voiced and voiceless consonants. You can further develop your English pronunciation by knowing the difference between voiced and voiceless consonants. For some words in English, the **verb** form ends with a **voiced** consonant sound and the noun form ends with a **voiceless** consonant sound.

Group work: Nouns and Verbs

Student A: Say a noun or verb from each pair of words below.
Student B: Say "noun" or "verb."

Nouns	Verbs
proof /f/	prove /v/
safe /f/	save /v/
use /s/	use /z/
advice /s/	advise /z/
excuse /s/	excuse /z/
belief /f/	believe /v/
relief /f/	relieve /v/
grief /f/	grieve /v/
device /s/	devise /z/

Culture Corner

Eating Etiquette

Billy Pham | www.billypham.com

Table manners play an important role in making a positive impression. Below are a list of Dos and Don'ts to make you feel comfortable when eating with Americans in public. Add your own Dos and Don'ts to the list below.

6

General Dos

- Try to have light conversation with everyone at the table.
- Do put your napkin in your lap. When you are finished with your dinner, place it loosely on the table, not on the plate and never on the chair.
- Do raise your hand and say, "Excuse me, please!" when you need help in a restaurant.
- Do assume each person will pay for their share of the bill when eating in a group unless someone clearly states they will pay. Likewise, many couples split the bill while dating. This tradition is called "going Dutch".
- ______________________________
- ______________________________
- ______________________________
- ______________________________

General Dos

- Don't eat too fast – take time to enjoy the food.
- Don't talk when your mouth is full of food.
- Don't chew with your mouth open.
- Don't place your elbows on the table and keep your left hand in your lap unless you are using it.
- Don't make loud eating noises such as slurping (e.g. soup) and burping.
- Don't blow your nose at the dinner table. Excuse yourself to visit the restroom. Wash your hands before returning to the dining room.
- Don't answer your phone during the meal.
- Don't floss, use a toothpick, and/or apply makeup at the table.
- Don't say that you're going the restroom. Instead, use "Excuse me" or "I'll be right back" before leaving the table.
- ______________________________
- ______________________________
- ______________________________
- ______________________________

Classroom Activity: Role-Play

A Night Out at a Fancy Restaurant in Dallas, Texas

A. Asking Questions

Eating out can be fun and satisfying, especially if ordering in English. What are two typical questions to ask a waiter at a nice restaurant?

1. ______________________________
2. ______________________________

What are two questions you might ask a friend at dinner?

1. ______________________________
2. ______________________________

6

B. Accidents Happen!

Billy Pham | www.billypham.com

Everybody wants to have a good time when they go out, but sometimes bad things happen to good people—even in nice restaurants!

Let's imagine this situation: Two friends are going to dinner, and they want to talk. At the restaurant, a new waiter has just started. He's very nervous. It's a busy night at a fashionable restaurant on Saturday night. Everybody wants to have a good time, but accidents do happen. Answer the questions and act in your own play. Have fun!

1. What will happen?
2. Who are the friends? What are their names?
3. What do they want to talk about?
4. What's the restaurant's name?
5. Where is the restaurant?
6. Why did they choose this restaurant?
7. Who is the new waiter? What is the waiter's name? What does the waiter look like? Why is the restaurant so busy?
8. What accidents will happen?
9. What happens next?
10. Can you create a fun skit?

Search & Share

Choosing a Local Restaurant

Student Name:______________________ Date:______________________

Jason Q. Tran | www.jasonqtran.com

Can you recommend a good place for dinner around here? Find and share a positive review for a local restaurant that you like. Pick a favorite local restaurant, do some research, and pick the best review— in English. Use this worksheet to tell us about the review.

Remember restaurant reviews should provide examples and details. Tell us about a special restaurant—in English—and help us find a place to eat delicious food.

6

Restaurant: ______________________ Location: ______________________

Reviewer: ______________________ Review: ______________________

1. Why did you pick this review?
2. How does the reviewer describe the restaurant? What kind of food does it serve?
3. When was the review written?
4. What do you know about the reviewer?
5. What does the reviewer say about the restaurant's atmosphere?
6. How did the reviewer describe the restaurant's service?
7. What did the reviewer eat?
8. What was the best part of the restaurant review?
9. Does the reviewer recommend the restaurant? Why?
10. How often have you been to the restaurant? What makes this restaurant special?

"One man's meat is another man's poison."
—Latin proverb

Chapter 7

Habits and Routines

> **"We first make our habits, then our habits make us."**
> —John Dryden (1631-1700), English playwright, translator and Poet Laureate

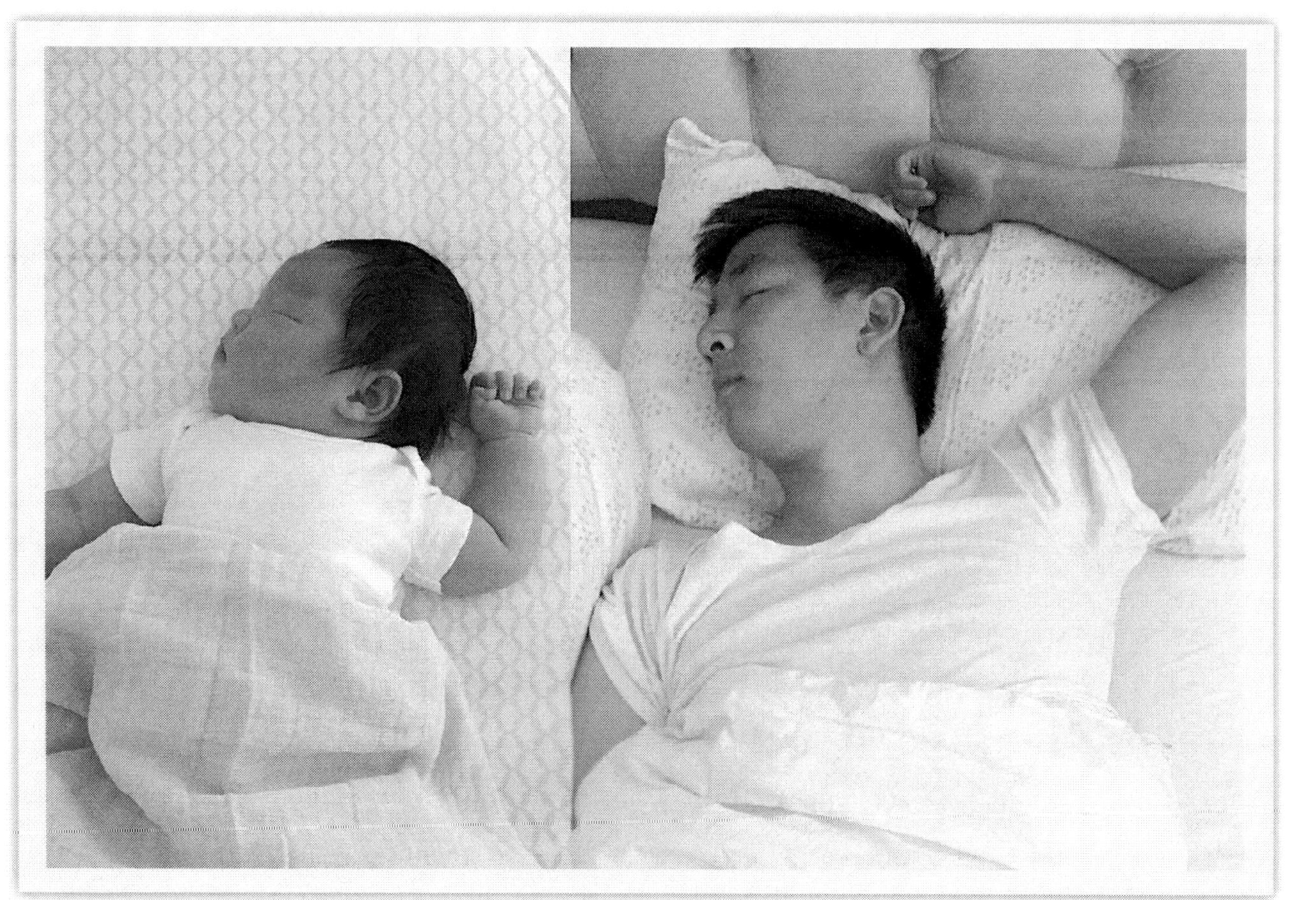

Photographer | Kim Ngo

Getting Started

Billy Pham | www.billypham.com

What do you usually do?

Directions:
In this fun activity, Student A will choose any word from the Habits and Routines list below. Student B will listen and use physical gestures—but NO voice—to "act out" the word. If Student B answers correctly, both students will switch rolls. If Student B guesses incorrectly, Student A will choose another phrase and Student B will be the "actor" again.

Habits and Routines

1. Brush teeth
2. Clean room
3. Comb hair
4. Cook dinner
5. Daydream
6. Do laundry
7. Drink lots of water
8. Eat vegetables
9. Exercise
10. Get dressed for work/school
11. Go to bed/sleep
12. Meet a friend
13. Sort mail
14. Study English
15. Take out the trash
16. Walk dog
17. Wash face
18. Watch TV
19. Go to the grocery store
20. Read book
21. Style hair
22. Take a walk
23. Wake up early
24. Wash dishes
25. Write a to-do list
26. Talk to a friend
27. ______________
28. ______________
29. ______________
30. ______________
31. ______________

Sharing Experiences

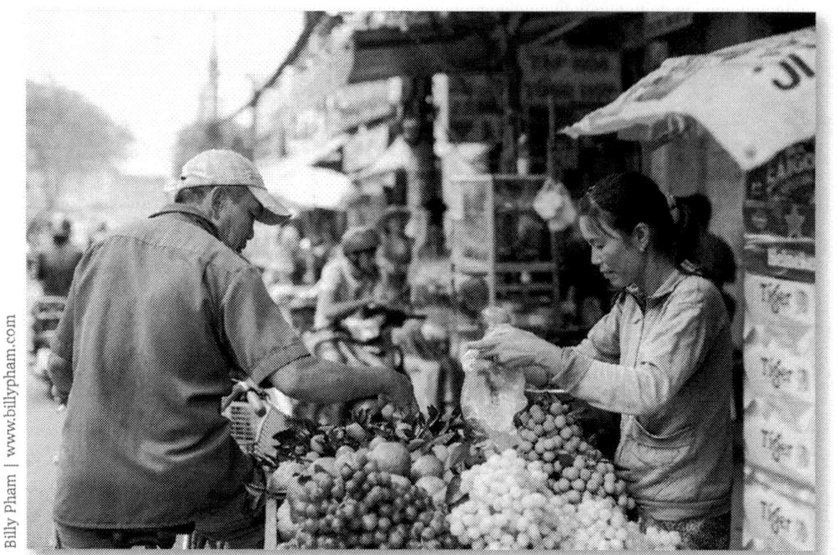

Billy Pham | www.billypham.com

Everybody eats. Food is both a necessity and a pleasure; it remains a safe and interesting way to learn more about people and cultures. Interview your partner and share your eating and drinking experiences.

7

1. How many hours of sleep do you usually get? Are you an "early bird" or a "night owl?"
2. What time do you usually get up in the morning? Do you use the alarm on your phone to wake you up?
3. Do you usually jump out of bed, or do you press the snooze button?
4. Can you describe your morning habits? Are you in a hurry? Do you have time to eat breakfast, walk your dog, or read the newspaper?
5. Do you have any bad habits? Can you tell me one bad habit?
6. Can you think of a few habits people often want to make or break for their New Year's resolutions?
7. How do you try to develop healthy habits?
8. What do you usually eat for breakfast? Do you eat on the run or do you skip breakfast?
9. How did you come to school today? Did you arrive by bus, by car, by bike, or on foot?
10. How long is your daily commute to work or school?
11. What are your shopping habits for clothes? Do you tend to buy the same type of clothes?
12. Can you describe your daily schedule? Do you have a favorite time of day?
13. What was your daily schedule like five years ago? How is it different now?
14. What tasks or chores have you put off or postponed?
15. Do you do many things at the last minute? Do you like to procrastinate? Why?

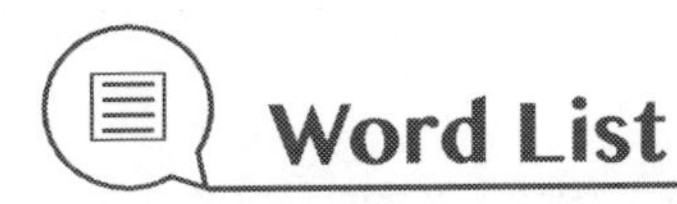

Word List

Which words do you already know? Underline them, and circle the words you are unsure about. Then review your answers with a partner.

Noun	Verb	Adjective
bargain /bo.gần/	**bargain** **/bo.gần/**	curious /khia.rì.ờs/
*consumer /khần.xu.mờ/	**discipline** **/đís.xịb.blìn/**	impulsive /ìm.pô.xịv/
discipline **/đís.xịb.blìn/**	***schedule** **/ske.jồ/**	oversleep /ô.vờ.slíb/
habit /ha.bịt/	*seek /sík/	**disciplined** **/đís.xịb.blìn/**
lifestyle /laiph.stai.ồ/		
***schedule** **/ske.jồ/**		
task /thás/		
*role /rôl/		

*Indicates words on the Academic Word List. See p.204 for all AWL words used in this book.

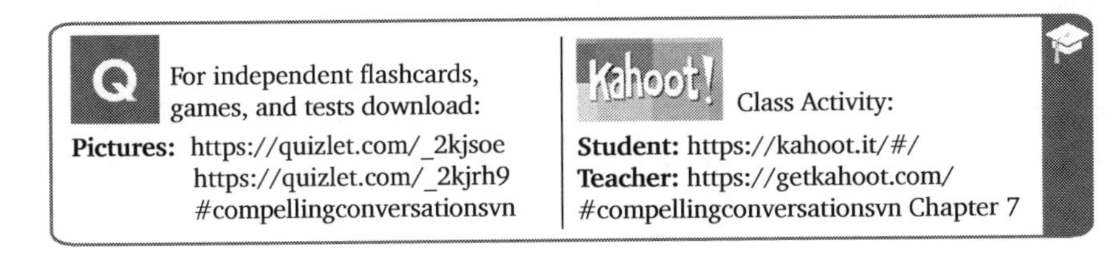

Expanding Vocabulary

Look at the definitions and example sentences below. Do the definitions match what you and your partner expected in the Word List? If not, what is different?

bargain [noun]: a good buy for the price.
[verb]: to try to buy an item at a cheaper price.

Ex: I like to shop for **bargains** in the markets, and often I bargain with sellers.

consumer [noun]: a person who buys products or services.

> Ex: **Consumers** like bargains where they can buy quality products at low prices.

curious [adjective]: an active desire to learn or know about things; strange or unusual.

> Ex: I am **curious** about your educational programs.
> Kiều Dung had a **curious** habit of stroking her eyebrow when she talked to me.

disciplined [adjective]: following a strict routine.

> Ex: You need a more **disciplined** approach to learn more and get better grades.

habit [noun]: repeated course of action developed over time; settled routine.

> Ex: By **habit** and self-discipline, he got up before dawn and worked until sunset.

impulsive [adjective]: to suddenly act.

7

> Ex: Khánh Điệp was **impulsive** and bought the expensive, new motorbike without telling her parents or knowing how to pay for gas.

lifestyle [noun]: the way a person leads their life.

> Ex: He kept a simple **lifestyle**: he ate healthy food, worked hard six days a week, and read poetry at night.

oversleep [verb]: to sleep late; to fail to wake up on time.

> Ex: I set two alarm clocks to be sure I wouldn't **oversleep** and miss my final examination at school.

role [noun]: proper place or function; a part played by an actor.

> Ex: What **role** does sleep play in staying healthy?

schedule [noun]: a timetable or a series of events.
[verb]: to make appointments.

> Ex: My **schedule** is full. Can we meet next week?
> I will **schedule** you with the doctor on Tuesday at 3:00.

seek [verb]: to search for, to try.

> Ex: We **seek** happiness, but we often feel stressed.

task [noun]: obligation, chore, something that must be done.

> Ex: What **tasks** do you have at work this week?

Asking Questions with New Vocabulary Words

A. Select five vocabulary words in this chapter and write a question for each word. Remember to start your question with a question word (Who, What, Where, When, Why, How, Is, Are, Do, Did, Does, etc.). You also want to end each question with a question mark (?). Underline each vocabulary word.

Example: *What is your schedule for next semester?*

1. ____________________
2. ____________________
3. ____________________
4. ____________________
5. ____________________

B. Take turns asking and answering questions with your partner or group members. Ask your instructor to give you feedback on your questions to check your English grammar.

Paraphrasing Proverbs

Read the following proverbs and discuss them with your partner. Write what you think they mean in the spaces provided. Circle your favorites. Explain your choices.

Vietnamese:

Smart birds sing wisdom. The wise speak gentle, soothing words.
"Chim khôn kêu tiếng rảnh rang. Người khôn nói tiếng dịu dàng, dễ nghe."
Meaning: ____________________

A clean house is fresh, a clean bowl is delicious rice.
"Nhà sạch thì mát, bát sạch ngon cơm."
Meaning: ____________________

Practice and you'll succeed, persevere and you'll be great.
"Luyện mãi thành tài, miệt mài tất giỏi."
Meaning: ____________________

International:

The more you chew your meat, the better it tastes; the more you speak, the lighter your heart becomes. —Korean
Meaning: ____________________

An old cat will never learn to dance. —Moroccan
Meaning: ______________________________

Habits are first cobwebs, then cables. —Spanish
Meaning: ______________________________

Love makes marriage possible, and habit makes it endurable. —American
Meaning: ______________________________

The fool in a hurry drinks his tea with chopsticks. —Chinese
Meaning: ______________________________

Remember

- Work hard
- Reflect
- Choose wisely

7 Building Words

Using the Old English Prefix "over-"

Prefix	Meaning	Example
over-	an excessive amount	"**Over**sleep" means to sleep more than needed or wanted.
over-	above/beyond	"**Over**see" means to supervise or direct.

The Old English prefix "over" is often used to convey "an excessive amount" or more of something than is really needed. For instance, the word "oversleep" means to sleep more than needed or wanted. Have you ever overslept? Remember, English is a living language. So many words that were started as two separate words become one word over time. Checking different dictionaries can sometimes also show different results.

Complete the chart below by following the example. Do the following mean "an excessive amount" or "above/beyond?" For the last two rows, add new base words.

Prefix	Base	New Word
over-	look	overlook
over-	see	
over-	seas	
over-	turn	
over-		
over-		

Complete the chart. Do the following mean "an excessive amount" or "above/beyond?"

Prefix	Base	New Word
over-	sleep	oversleep
over-	achiever	
over-	active	
over-	charge	
over-	confident	
over-	do	
over-	drive	
over-	pay	
over-	due	
over-	use	
over-	step	
over-	take	
over-	weight	
over-		
over-		

A. Select four words from the above chart and create a question for your partner. Remember to start your question with a question word (Who, What, Where, When, Why, How, Is, Are, Do, Did, Does, etc.). You also want to end each question with a question mark (?). Underline each vocabulary word.

1. ______________________________
2. ______________________________
3. ______________________________
4. ______________________________

7

B. Take turns asking and answering questions with your partner. Ask your instructor to give you feedback on your questions to check your English grammar.

Discussing Quotations

In your small groups, take turns reading these quotations out loud and discuss them. Do you agree with the quotation? Disagree? Why? Mark your opinion. Afterwards, pick a favorite quotation. Remember to give a reason or an example.

1. **"Nothing is in reality either pleasant or unpleasant by nature; but all things become so through habit."**
—Epictetus (55–135), Greek stoic philosopher ☐**Agree** ☐**Disagree**

2. **"Men's natures are alike; it is their habits that separate them."**
—Confucius (551–479 B.C.E.) Chinese philosopher ☐**Agree** ☐**Disagree**

7

3. **"We are what we repeatedly do. Excellence, then, is not an act, but a habit."**
—Aristotle (384–322 B.C.E.), Greek philosopher ☐**Agree** ☐**Disagree**

4. **"The chains of habit are too weak to be felt until they are too strong to be broken."**
—Dr. Samuel Johnson (1709–1784), English author ☐**Agree** ☐**Disagree**

5. **"Habit for him was all the test of truth; 'It must be right: I've done it from my youth.'"**
—George Crabbe (1754–1832), English poet ☐**Agree** ☐**Disagree**

6. **"The perpetual obstacle to human advancement is custom."**
—John Stuart Mill (1806–1873), English philosopher ☐**Agree** ☐**Disagree**

7. **"Nothing so needs reforming as other people's habits."**
—Mark Twain (1835–1910), American writer ☐**Agree** ☐**Disagree**

8. **"Any man who reads too much and uses his own brain too little falls into lazy habits of thinking."**
—Albert Einstein (1879–1955), physicist, Nobel Prize winner (1921) and Time magazine's "Man of the 20th Century" ☐**Agree** ☐**Disagree**

9. **"For many, negative thinking is a habit, which over time, becomes an addiction."**
—Peter McWilliams (1949–2000), American author ☐ **Agree** ☐ **Disagree**

10. **"The unfortunate thing about this world is that good habits are so much easier to give up than bad ones."**
—Somerset Maugham (1874–1965), English writer ☐ **Agree** ☐ **Disagree**

Discussion: Which was your favorite quote? Why?

____

____

____

The Conversation Continues

Let's continue to explore topics related to habits and routines with one or two classmates. Use complete sentences to respond.

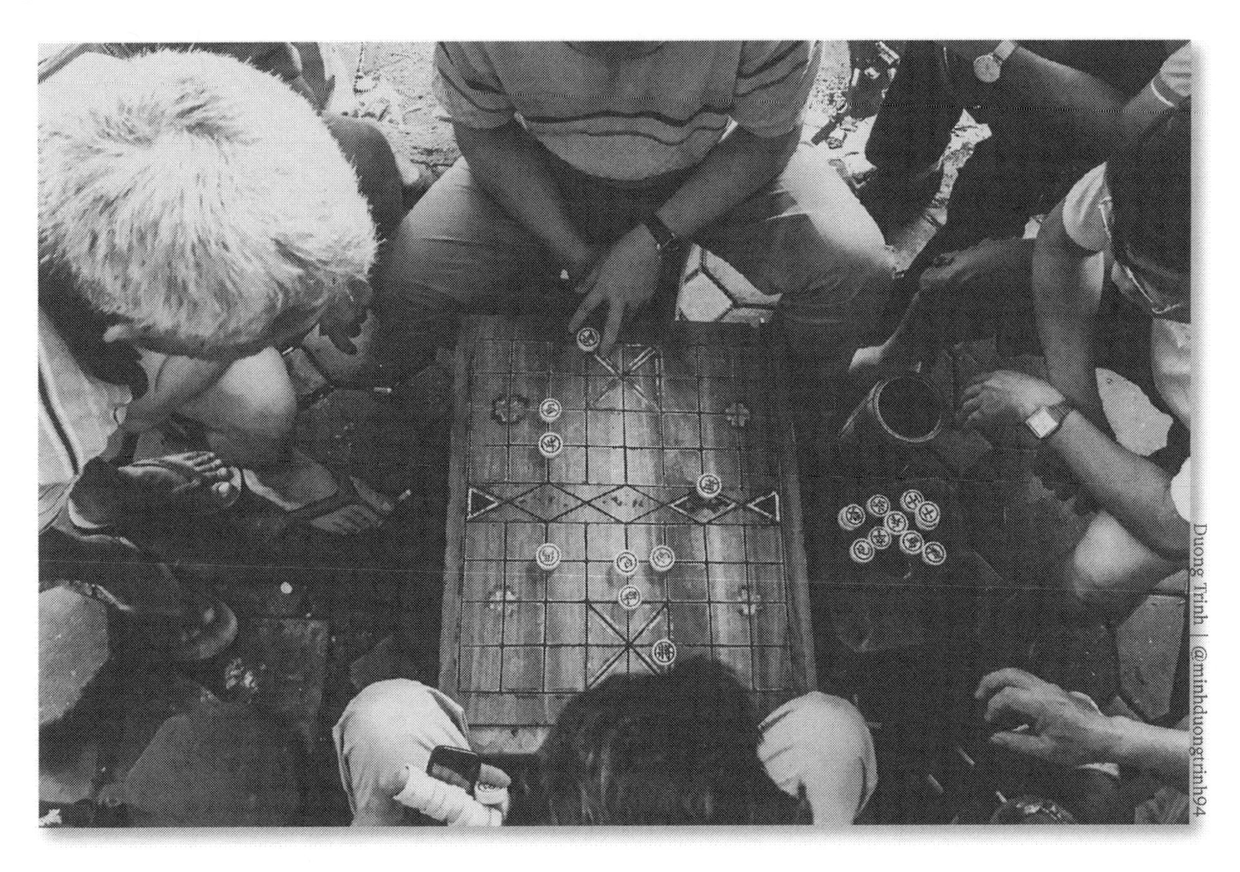

Duong Trinh | @minhduongtrinh94

1. Where do you go to find bargains when shopping?
2. What are your TV viewing habits? Online sufing habit? Which TV or online shows do you like to watch?
3. How often do you check your email? Facebook? Instagram? Snapchat? The Internet?
4. How can you develop a good habit?
5. What are some dangerous or unhealthy habits? How can you get rid of a bad habit?
6. Do children learn habits at home or at school? Why?
7. In what ways are you self-disciplined? How do you stay motivated?
8. Are you sometimes lazy? How?
9. Do you tend to see the glass as half-full or half-empty? Are you more of an optimist or a pessimist? Why?
10. When do you feel most alive? Why?
11. What are some of your healthier habits?
12. Do you have less healthy habits too? What?
13. How do your habits compare to your parents' habits at your age?
14. What are you some unusual habits that you've seen?
15. Looking ahead, how would you like to change your habits in the next five years?

Pronunciation Corner

Introducing Vowels

Learning how to pronounce vowels correctly can really help listeners understand you better when speaking English. As you may know, Vietnamese has a very limited number of vowel sounds. Therefore, many native Vietnamese speakers sometimes find it challenging to master the wide variety of vowel sounds in English. In English, there are five vowel letters, but many vowel sounds. In the following task, you will learn and practice common vowel sounds.

Group work: Use the "buttons" below to give and get phone numbers of three classmates.

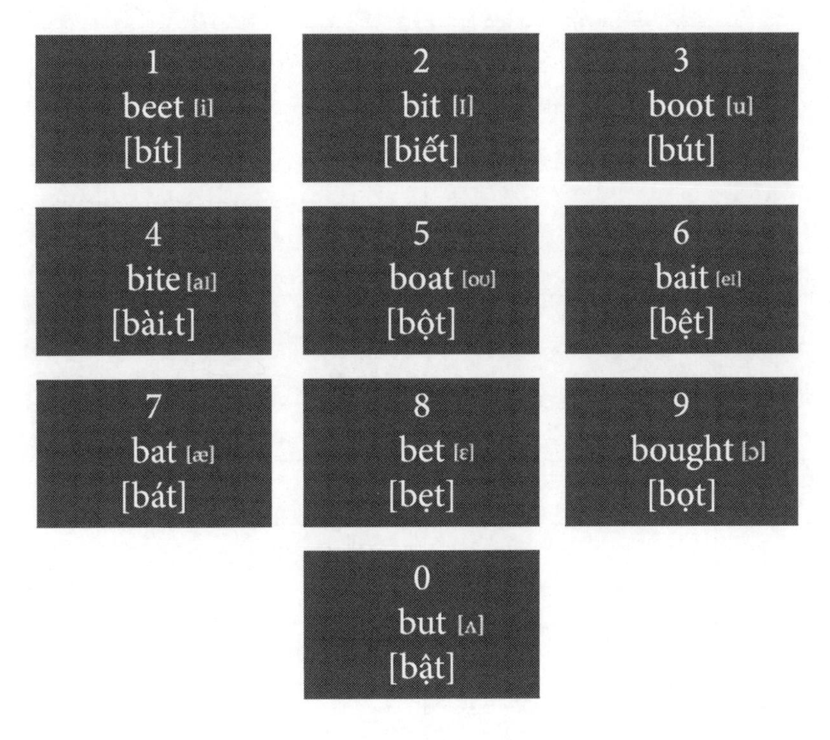

Classmate: ______________________ Phone number: ______________________

Classmate: ______________________ Phone number: ______________________

Classmate: ______________________ Phone number: ______________________

Culture Corner

Tip and Gratuity

Clara Hutzler | www.hellosuitcase.com

A tip or gratuity is additional money given to certain employees for their service, a standard in the U.S. Tip and gratuity are used interchangeably with gratuity slightly more formal. Keep in mind that the amount of tip varies depending on the level of service and the type of the business.

Occupation	Tipping Amount
Taxi Driver	15% of total fare If the driver was especially helpful or got you to your destination quicker than you expected, give a 20% tip.
Hotel Bellhop	$1.00 for helping you with your luggage or bags.
Coatroom Attendant	$1.00 per coat
Hairdressers/Barbers/Spa employees	15-20% of cost of services
Valet Parking Attendant	$2.00-$7.00 per car
Waiters/Waitresses/Bartenders	15% of total bill for average service, 20% or more for very good service, and no less than 10% for poor service
Hotel Housekeepers	$2-5 per night
Carrier, Delivery Professional, Driver (e.g. pizza, flowers)	10-15% of the order If it was a difficult delivery (e.g. stairs, bad weather), give a 20% tip.

Activity 1: Do not tip or give gifts to government employees because this can be categorized as a "bribe" and is a serious crime. Government employees include the following. With a partner, think of other government employees you should not "tip."

- Customs or immigration officials
- Driver's test examiners
- ______________________________
- ______________________________
- ______________________________
- ______________________________

Activity 2: With a partner, discuss the following questions.

1. Do you usually leave a tip?
2. How much are you supposed to tip different people?
3. Is tipping common in your country?
4. Why is it important to leave tips?
5. Can you think of some places where tipping is required?
6. Can you think of some places where tipping is optional?
7. Can you think of some places where tipping is not necessary?

Classroom Activity:

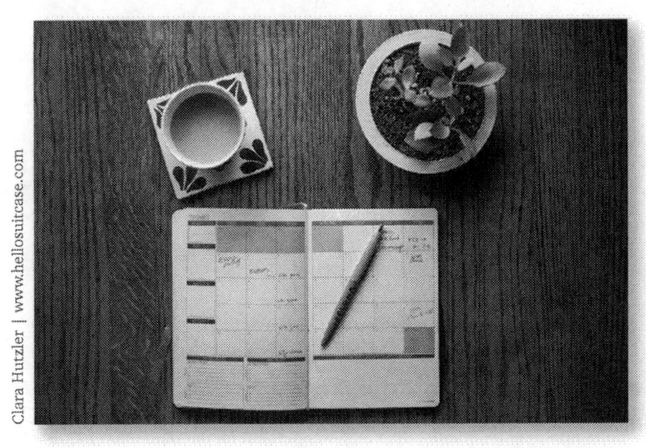
Clara Hutzler | www.hellosuitcase.com

What's your schedule like?

Student Name: ____________________

Date: ____________________

Write down your typical schedule for the week. Remember to include meals and meetings. Share your schedule with your conversation partner.

	Monday	Tuesday	Wednesday	Thursday	Friday	Saturday	Sunday
6:00 a.m.							
7:00 a.m.							
8:00 a.m.							
9:00 a.m.							
10:00 a.m.							
11:00 a.m.							
noon							
1:00 p.m.							
2:00 p.m.							
3:00 p.m.							
4:00 p.m.							
5:00 p.m.							
6:00 p.m.							
7:00 p.m.							
8:00 p.m.							
9:00 p.m.							
10:00 p.m.							
11:00 p.m.							
Midnight							

7

Search & Share

How do you spend your time?

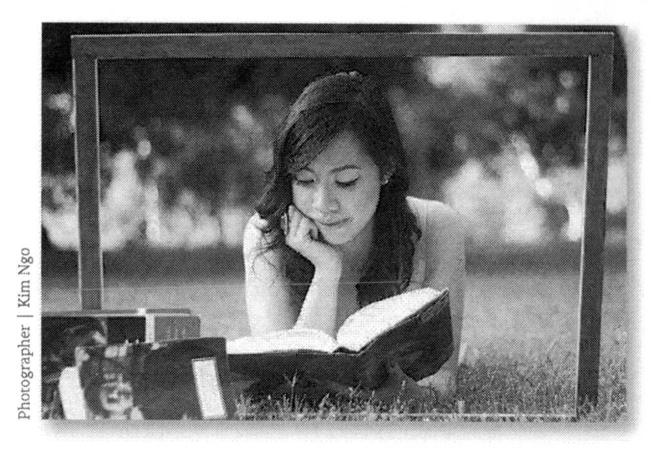
Photographer | Kim Ngo

Student Name: ____________________

Date: ____________________

Enter the amount of time you spend on each of the following activities on a typical weekday. Use your best estimate or guess for each category.

Activity 1:

7

Activity	Hours	Minutes
sleeping		
eating and drinking housework/cleaning up		
attending classes		
working at a job commuting/driving		
playing sports and exercising		
using your cell phone		
watching TV		
attending religious services/praying		
socializing		
relaxing		

For any of the above activities, would you say that you spend more or less time on it compared to yourself a year ago? Why?

Activity 2: Disscuss your activities in small groups.

> **"All the treasures of the earth cannot bring back one lost moment."**
> —French proverb

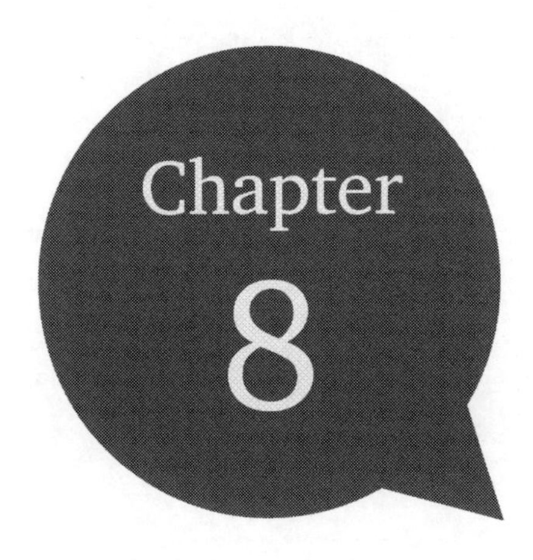

Being Yourself

"**Be yourself. Everyone else is taken.**"
– Oscar Wilde (1854-1900), Irish playwright and author

Getting Started

Photographer | Tung Phan

What does your name mean?

Directions:
Use a dictionary, Google, or any other resource. Find and write down an adjective that begins with each letter of your first name and that describes who you are. Share with a classmate, write notes, and prepare to introduce your partner to the class.

Example:

Believable
Incredible
Leading
Lively
Young

Sharing Experiences

From consulting charts and reading palms to taking personality tests and reading self-help books, people love to describe themselves.

Photographer | Tung Phan

1. How would you describe yourself as a child? Why?
2. Are you shy or outgoing? When are you most outgoing?
3. Are you daring or cautious? In what ways?
4. Are you usually patient or impatient? Can you give an example?
5. Are you quiet or talkative? When are you most talkative? Least talkative?

6 Would you call yourself a leader or a follower? Why?
7 Are you generous or selfish? Are you sometimes too selfish or overly generous?
8 In what ways are you rigid? In what ways are you flexible?
9 In what ways are you traditional? In what ways are you modern?
10 If pessimistic is 1 and optimistic is 10, what would your number be on the scale? Why did you decide on that number?
11 On a scale of 1-10, how assertive are you?
12 Is your personality more like your mother or your father? In what ways?
13 Which color would you use to describe your personality?
14 Which animal would you use to describe yourself? Tiger? Mouse? Why?
15 Which three adjectives best describe your personality today?

Word List

Which words do you already know? Underline them, and circle the words you are unsure about. Then review your answers with a partner.

8

Noun	Verb	Adjective
character /khe.rạc.tờ/	nurture /nơ.chờ/	*accurate /ác.cơ.rịt/
optimist /ób.tờ.mís.tịc/		*flexible /phles.sơ.bồ/
pessimist /pés.sơ.mìs/		generous /jen.nờ.rầs/
*potential /pồ.then.chồ/		**patient /pêy.shịnt/**
patient /pêy.shịnt/		*rigid /rê.jịd/
		talkative /thók.ca.thiph/
		*positive /po.zi.thìv/

*Indicates words on the Academic Word List. See p.204 for all AWL words used in this book.

For independent flashcards, games, and tests download:
Pictures: https://quizlet.com/_2kk01w
https://quizlet.com/_2kjthi
#compellingconversationsvn

Class Activity:
Student: https://kahoot.it/#/
Teacher: https://getkahoot.com/
#compellingconversationsvn Chapter 8

Expanding Vocabulary

Look at the definitions and example sentences below. Do the definitions match what you and your partner expected in the Word List? If not, what is different?

accurate [adjective]: correct, getting the facts right.

> Ex: Scientists, engineers, and doctors must be **accurate**.

character [noun]: one's personality and values; moral sense; a figure in fiction or theater.

> Ex: Anh Khuê showed her **character** at work.
> Oliver Twist is one of my favorite **characters** in English literature.

flexible [adjective]: loose, bending; willing to change.

> Ex: Trí Dũng is **flexible** and can work either Friday or Saturday.

generous [adjective]: giving, sharing with others.

> Ex: A good sister is **generous** with her time and helps her family.

8

nurture [verb]: to take care of another; to care for or help someone in need.

> Ex: Parents **nurture** their children and guide them in their lives.

patient [adjective]: able to wait calmly, not in a hurry.
[noun]: a person receiving medical treatment.

> Ex: A **patient** man can calmly wait for a late bus.
> The doctor prescribed medicine for her **patient**.

optimist [noun]: someone who see the positive side and believes things will get better.

> Ex: She saw the glass as "half-full," which made her an **optimist**.

pessimist [noun]: one who has a negative view and thinks things will get worse.

> Ex: He saw the glass as "half-empty," which made him a **pessimist**.

positive [adjective]: optimistic; certainty that something is true.

> Ex: It's important to maintain a **positive** attitude in times of difficulty.

potential [noun]: possibility capable of becoming reality.

> **Ex:** Every student in our class has the **potential** to be successful if they put time and effort into studying.
> Her **potential** knows no limits.

rigid [adjective]: unwilling to change; inflexible.

> **Ex:** Minh Tuấn is so **rigid** that he will not even listen to other people.

talkative [adjective]: verbal; engages in constant or non-stop conversation.

> **Ex:** Bảo Sơn becomes **talkative** when he relaxes with his friends.

? Asking Questions with New Vocabulary Words

A. Select five vocabulary words in this chapter and write a question for each word. Remember to start your question with a question word (Who, What, Where, When, Why, How, Is, Are, Do, Did, Does, etc.). End each question with a question mark (?). Underline each vocabulary word.

Example: *Are you feeling optimistic today?*

1. ________________________________
2. ________________________________
3. ________________________________
4. ________________________________
5. ________________________________

B. Take turns asking and answering questions with your partner or group members.

8

Remember

- Respect yourself
- Be yourself
- Create your future

Paraphrasing Proverbs

Read the following proverbs and discuss them with your partner. Write what you think they mean in the spaces provided. Circle your favorites. Explain your choices.

Vietnamese:

The leopard cannot change its spots.
"Giang sơn dễ đổi, bản tính khó dời."
Meaning:

Practice results in success. Perseverance results in greatness.
"Luyện mãi thành tài, miệt mài tất giỏi."
Meaning:

First is manners, second is knowledge.
"Tiên học lễ, hậu học văn."
Meaning:

International:

Character is destiny. —Greek
Meaning:

Trust yourself. —American
Meaning:

The more noble, the more humble. —Chinese
Meaning:

A light heart lives long. —English
Meaning:

A pretty being is better than being pretty. —English
Meaning:

Remember

What do you like about yourself? Write a postcard to a friend describing your strongest traits.

To

Building Words

Adding the Latin Prefix "in-"

We have already learned that the common prefix "ex-" means out or outside in Chapter 3. Do you remember these words?

Exterior
Exclude
Exhibit
Exhale

We sometimes see the opposite of these words using the prefix "in-." Can you guess what the prefix "in" means? Here's a hint: the opposite of the word "exterior" is "interior."

Prefix	Meaning	Example
in-	in	Inside. The words "**in**side" and "**in**doors" are physical descriptions where the prefix "in" literally means "in."
in-	not	The prefix "in" can also be used to mean "not" as in the words "**in**accurate" and "**in**complete."

8

Complete the chart. Do the following mean "inside" or "not?" For the last two rows, add new root words.

Prefix	Base	New Word
in-	terior	*interior*
in-	clude	
in-	hibit	
in-	side	
in-	sight	
in-	trovert	
in-		
in-		

Complete the chart. Do the following mean "inside" or "not"? For the last two rows, add new root words.

Prefix	Base	New Word
in-	accurate	*inaccurate*
in-	flexible	
in-		
in-		

Note the prefix "in-" becomes "im-" before the letters "m," "b," and "p." Complete the chart. For the last two rows, add new root words.

Prefix	Base	New Word
im-	mature	*immature*
im-	press	
im-	plicit	
im-	pose	
im-		
im-		

8

A. Select four words from the above chart and create a question for your partner. Remember to start your question with a question word (Who, What, Where, When, Why, How, Is, Are, Do, Did, Does, etc.). End each question with a question mark (?). Underline each vocabulary word.

1. ______________________________
2. ______________________________
3. ______________________________
4. ______________________________

B. Take turns asking and answering questions with your partner. Ask your instructor to give you feedback on your questions to check your English grammar.

Discussing Quotations

In your small groups, take turns reading these quotations out loud and discuss them. Do you agree with the quotation? Disagree? Why? Mark your opinion. Afterwards, pick a favorite quotation. Remember to give a reason or an example.

1. **"Know thyself."**
   —Socrates (470-399 B.C.E.), Greek philosopher ☐ Agree ☐ Disagree

2. **"The man of character bears the accidents of life with dignity and grace, making the best of circumstances."**
   —Aristotle (384–322 B.C.E.), Greek philosopher ☐ Agree ☐ Disagree

3. **"This above all: To thine own self be true, And it must follow, as the night the day, Thou canst not then be false to any man."**
   —William Shakespeare (1564-1616), English poet ☐ Agree ☐ Disagree

4. **"Character is much easier kept than recovered."**
   —Thomas Paine (1737–1809), American writer ☐ Agree ☐ Disagree

5. **"It is absurd to divide people into good and bad. People are either charming or tedious."**
   —Oscar Wilde (1856–1900), Irish writer ☐ Agree ☐ Disagree

6. **"Some people with great virtues are disagreeable, while others with great vice are delightful."**
   —Francois de la Rochefoucauld (1613—1680), French philosopher ☐ Agree ☐ Disagree

7. **"Man's main task in life is to give birth to himself, to become what he potentially is. The most important product of his effort is his own personality."**
   —Erich Fromm (1900–1980), German-American psychologist ☐ Agree ☐ Disagree

8. **"Generous people are rarely mentally ill people."**
   —Karl Menninger (1893–1990), American psychiatrist ☐ Agree ☐ Disagree

9. **"The easiest kind of relationship for me is with ten thousand people. The hardest is with one."**
   —Joan Baez (1941 -), American singer ☐ Agree ☐ Disagree

10. **"Dwell in possibility."**
    —Emily Dickinson (1830-1886), American poet ☐ Agree ☐ Disagree

Discussion: Which was your favorite quote? Why?

____

____

____

The Conversation Continues

Let's continue to explore topics related to being you with one or two classmates. Use complete sentences to respond.

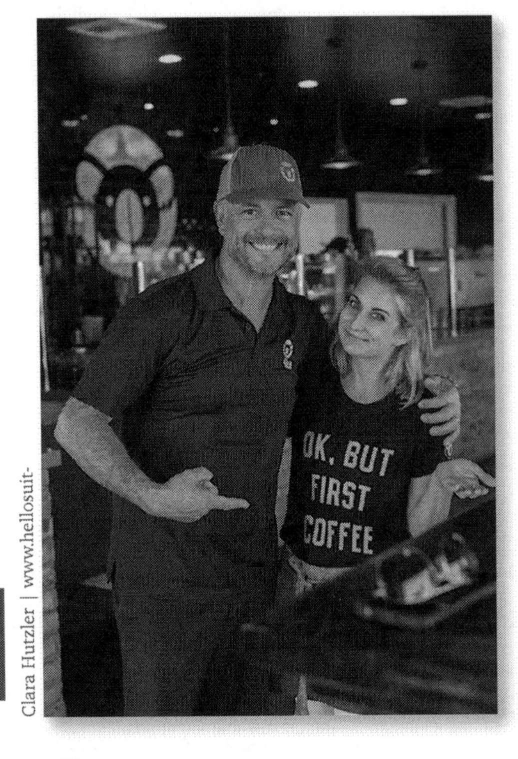

Clara Hutzler | www.hellosuit-

8

1. Do you think our personalities are set when we are born? Why?
2. Can we change our personalities? How?
3. Do you think opposites attract? Why?
4. Which three words would you use to describe your best friend's personality?
5. How are your personalities similar? How are your personalities different?
6. Are you primarily an extrovert or an introvert? Why do you think so?
7. What is your astrology sign? Is the description accurate of your personality?
8. Which three qualities do you think of as feminine?
9. Which three qualities do you think of as masculine?
10. If you had been born in another country, do you think your personality would be different? How?
11. Can growing up in poverty influence someone's personality? How?
12. Would being born in extreme wealth influence your personality? How?
13. What makes you happy? Angry? Embarrassed? Sad?
14. What is the difference between personality and character?
15. What are your best qualities? Why?

Pronunciation Corner

/æ/ and /ʌ/

In this lesson, we will specifically focus on the difference between the vowel /æ/ "ah" in a word like [cat] and /ʌ/ "uh" in a word like [cut]. To make the /æ/ sound, you have to drop your tongue, tighten your jaw, and pull your mouth back in a half-smile.

The /ʌ/ sound is the most common sound in English. Relax every muscle in your face and throat, and let the sound come out. That is the /ʌ/ sound. You might find looking in a mirror helpful for this exercise.

Pair work: Do we match?

In the following activity, Student A will read #1 from his list and Student B will read #1 from his list. Listen carefully to each other and see if you are saying the same or different word from your partner. Remember to fold the page in two and cover your partner's word list.

	Student A	Student B
1.	bat	but
2.	cup	cup
3.	match	munch
4.	fun	fan
5.	bag	bag
6.	track	truck
7.	slum	slam
8.	mad	mad
9.	stub	stub
10.	cat	cut

Culture Corner

Gift Giving

Americans generally give gifts for birthdays, anniversaries, weddings, and major holidays, such as Christmas. A gift can vary from a simple card with a personal note to something fancier depending on your relationship with the receiver and the occasion. Keep in mind that presents and cards are often opened once received and frequently in front of other friends, coworkers, and relatives.

Clara Hutzler | www.hellosuitcase.com

Someone's Home

When invited to someone's home for dinner, it is polite to bring something small such as a box of chocolates, a bottle of wine, or a potted plant or flowers for the hostess.

Wedding

It is common for Americans to do a gift registry for weddings and showers (e.g. baby, bridal). A gift registry is when the person registers with the store the kind of gifts that they are interested in receiving.

When you go to the store, you can look up the person in the Gift Registry to get ideas about what they are looking for and, possibly, what other people have already purchased for the couple so you don't buy the same thing twice. This approach makes the gift buying easier because it guarantees that you can choose a gift that the couple need or want.

Activity 1: With a partner, discuss the similarities and differences of gift giving in the U.S and another country you have lived in or visited.

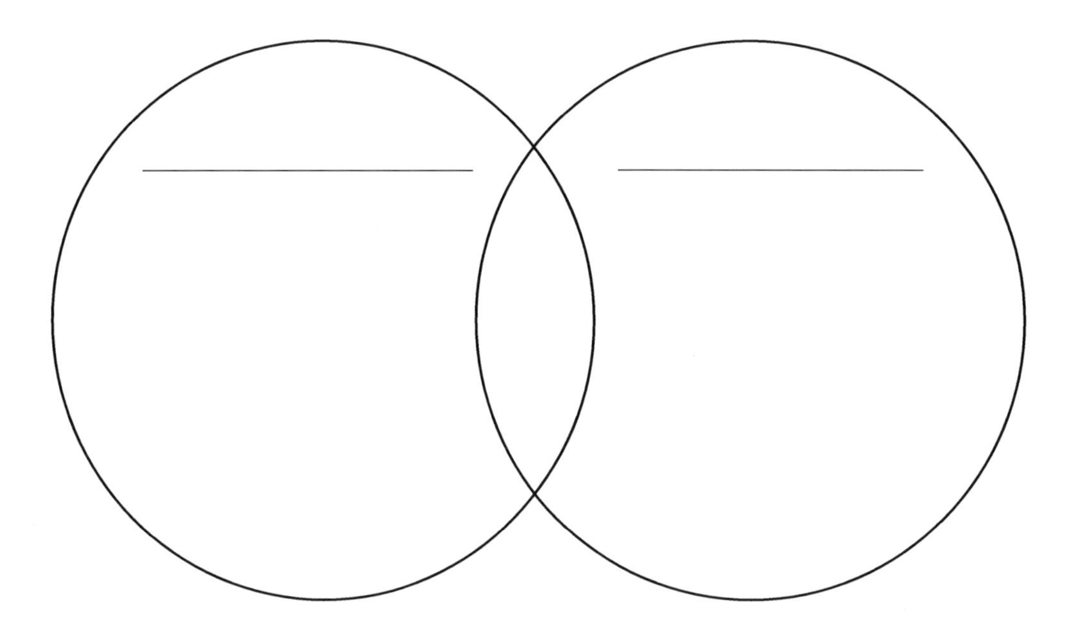

Activity 2: With a partner, discuss the following questions related to gift giving.

- What kinds of gifts to do you usually give?
- When do you usually receive gifts?
- Have you ever received a gift that you didn't like? What did you do with that gift?
- How do you thank someone who gave you a gift?

Search & Share

A Famous Person You Admire

Student Name:______________________ Date:______________________

Which famous person do you respect and look up to? For better or for worse, many Americans often pride themselves on their individualism. Outstanding individuals often believe they have made crucial decisions that led to their future success. Find a video about someone you admire. Who is this person? What did they do? How did they create a meaningful life? Learn more about a personal hero by watching a documentary or news feature. Be ready to discuss the video about your hero with your classmates.

1. Whom did you choose as a personal hero?
2. What video or documentary did you find?
3. Can you describe the person's background or childhood?
4. Did the main person or character face a problem? What was it?
5. What were some important decisions that this person made?
6. What obstacles did this person overcome?
7. What were some achievements or highlights of their life?
8. What was the most interesting part of the biography for you? Why?
9. Do you consider this person to be a hero? Why?
10. How would you rate the video on a scale of 1–5, with 5 being the highest? Why?

8

"Those who say that we're in a time when there are no heroes just don't know where to look."
—Ronald Reagan (1911-2004), 40th U.S. President

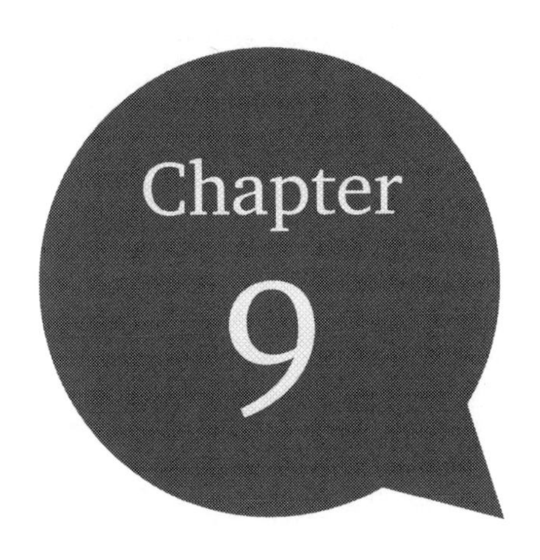

Staying Healthy

> **"Early to bed and early to rise makes a man healthy, wealthy and wise."**
> —Benjamin Franklin (1706-1790), American statesman

Getting Started

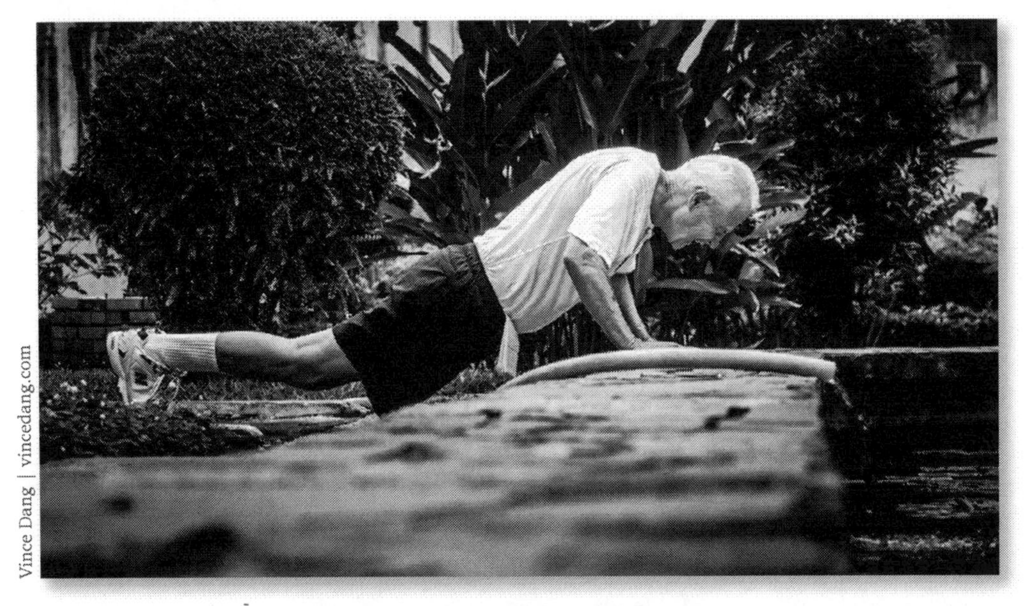

Vince Dang | vincedang.com

What's my health problem?

Directions:
Choose a common health problem below. Give advice to how to treat the problem to your partner. Continue to give advice until your partner is able to correctly guess the health problem.

- Allergies
- Back ache
- Bloody nose
- Broken arm
- Broken leg
- Bruise
- Cough
- Cut
- Diabetes
- Dizzy
- Earache
- Faint
- Fever
- Headache
- Heart attack
- Itch
- Obesity
- Runny nose
- Shivery
- Sneeze
- Sore throat
- Stomach ache
- Stuffy nose
- Swollen finger
- Toothache
- Flu

Sharing Experiences

Sometimes it is easier to talk the talk than walk the walk when it comes to staying healthy. Interview your partner and exchange health tips.

Vince Dang | vincedang.com

Walking the Walk

1. What are some signs of being healthy?
2. What do your friends do to stay healthy?
3. What are some other things that people can do to feel healthy?

9

4. Have your health habits changed in the last few years? How?
5. What is something that many people should do, but don't do to stay healthy?
6. Do you know any home remedies for common ailments? Old family remedies?
7. How do you treat a sore throat? Minor cut? Headaches?
8. What are some causes of back pain? What are some remedies?
9. Do you take daily vitamins? Which ones? Why?
10. What's the difference between over-the-counter drugs and prescription drugs?
11. How often do you wash your hands? What other precautions do you take to prevent the spread of germs?
12. Do you eat healthy food? Do you have any unhealthy eating habits?
13. Do you enjoy smoking? What are some of the dangers of smoking?
14. How much sleep do you usually get? Is your sleep restful, or do you toss and turn? Can you share ideas on how to sleep better?
15. How often do you feel tired or exhausted? What can you do to feel more energetic?

Word List

9 Which words do you already know? Underline them, and circle the words you are unsure about. Then review your answers with a partner.

Noun	Verb	Adjective
exercise **/és.sờ.xaiz/**	**exercise** **/és.sờ.xaiz/**	*medical /me.đi.cồ/
germ /jơm/	overcome /ô.vờ.khăm/	
medication /me.đa.khê.sần/	prevent /prì.vent/	
operation /ób.bơ.rê.sần/	**remedy** **/re.me.đì/**	
prescription / prì.scrít.sần/	*recover /rì.khơ.vờ/	
prevention /prì.ven.chần/		
symptom /xim.tầm/		
remedy **/re.me.đì/**		

*Indicates words on the Academic Word List. See p.204 for all AWL words used in this book.

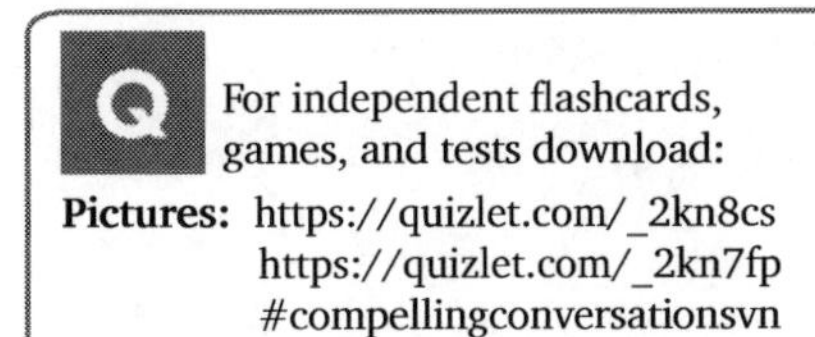

For independent flashcards, games, and tests download:

Pictures: https://quizlet.com/_2kn8cs
https://quizlet.com/_2kn7fp
#compellingconversationsvn

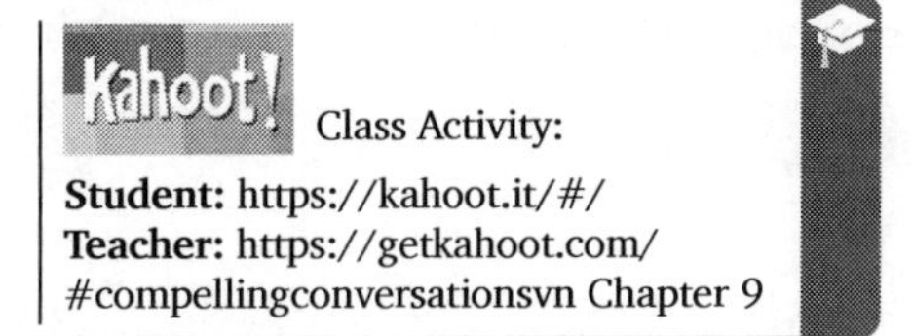

Class Activity:

Student: https://kahoot.it/#/
Teacher: https://getkahoot.com/
#compellingconversationsvn Chapter 9

Expanding Vocabulary

Look at the definitions and example sentences below. Do the definitions match what you and your partner expected in the Word List? If not, what is different?

exercise [noun]: physical activity to maintain good health.
[verb]: to be physically active; to perform activities well.

> Ex: I get my daily **exercise** by bicycling to work.
> Vĩnh Sơn **exercises** good judgment and seldom makes mistakes.

germ [noun]: a tiny organism that can cause illness, such as a virus or bacteria.

> Ex: **Germs** in undercooked food can cause you to get sick.

medication [noun]: a pill or other treatment designed to cure an illness.

> Ex: If he won't take his **medication**, his condition will probably get worse.

9

medical [adjective]: relating to the use of medicine to treat ailments and injuries.

> Ex: It's considered healthy to receive a **medical** check-up at least once a year.

operation [noun]: surgery; a medical procedure that cuts into and opens up the body;
a company or business action.

> Ex: It took Ngọc six weeks to recover from the medical **operation** performed by her doctor.
> Hồng manages the department and runs the entire **operation**, beginning to end.

overcome [verb]: to achieve your goals despite having to face difficult challenges along the

> Ex: Thục Uyên **overcame** a slow start to win the 200 meter race.
> "We shall **overcome**" was a key phrase of Dr. Martin Luther King, the African-American civil rights leader and Nobel Prize winner.

prescription [noun]: a written form signed by a doctor authorizing the purchase of medicine.

> **Ex:** Dr. Tùng wrote the **prescription** so the patient could get his medicine.

prevent [verb]: to stop something from taking place, to keep it from happening.

> **Ex:** Trọng Vinh took his medicine for 10 days to **prevent** his illness from returning.

prevention [noun]: stopping something from happening.

> **Ex:** "**Prevention** is better than medication" is a nursing slogan.

recover [verb]: to return to normal health or circumstances after illness or troubled times.

> **Ex:** He **recovered** from his illness rather quickly.

remedy [noun]: a medicine or treatment that relieves or cures a disease or symptom.
[verb]: to cure.

> **Ex:** Aspirin is a common **remedy** for headaches, but other remedies exist, too.

symptom [noun]: a sign of a disease or disorder; visible proof some other problem exists.

> **Ex:** The doctor recognized the fever and cough as classic flu **symptoms**.

? Asking Questions with New Vocabulary Words

A. Select five vocabulary words in this chapter and write a question for each word. Remember to start your question with a question word (Who, What, Where, When, Why, How, Is, Are, Do, Did, Does, etc.). You also want to end each question with a question mark (?). Underline each vocabulary word.

Example: *How often do you exercise?*

1. ______________________________
2. ______________________________
3. ______________________________
4. ______________________________
5. ______________________________

B. Take turns asking and answering questions with your partner or group members. Ask your instructor to give you feedback on your questions to check your English grammar.

Paraphrasing Proverbs

Read the following proverbs and discuss them with your partner. Write what you think they mean in the spaces provided. Circle your favorites. Explain your choices.

Vietnamese:

Rice is medicine for the body. Eating at the right time maintains balance and durability.
"Cơm là món thuốc nuôi thân. Ăn đúng giờ giấc cân bằng dẻo dai."
Meaning:________________________

One smile is the same as ten vitamin pills.
"Một nụ cười bằng mười thang thuốc bổ."
Meaning:________________________

There is no beauty like the beauty of muscle.
"Không vẻ đẹp nào đẹp bằng sự cuồn cuộn của cơ bắp."
Meaning:________________________

International:

An apple a day keeps the doctor away. —English
Meaning:________________________

9

A sick person is a prisoner. —Yemenite
Meaning:________________________

Nature, time, and patience are the three great physicians. —Irish
Meaning:________________________

Old age is a thousand headaches. —Persian
Meaning:________________________

Let a smile be your umbrella. —English
Meaning:________________________

On Your Own

List your top five tips for staying healthy and happy. Prepare to share your practical health advice with the class.

1. ________________________
2. ________________________
3. ________________________
4. ________________________
5. ________________________

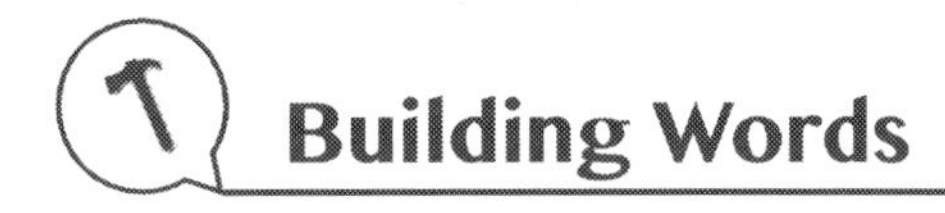

Building Words

Adding the Latin Suffix "-ity"

Suffix	Meaning	Example
-ity	condition/state	The adjective "able" becomes the noun "abil**ity**" by adding the suffix "**ity**." What's her "abil**ity**?"

Here are some common nouns that end in "ity." Do you know these 25 words? Can you identify the root word? Circle the words that you are unsure of and discuss with your partner. Note that all these words are nouns ending in the suffix "ity." If you see a word ending in "ity," you should recognize that it a noun.

Ability	Clarity	Equality	Intensity	Rigidity
Activity	Conformity	Fertility	Obesity	Sanity
Anxiety	Creativity	Flexibility	Personality	Security
Capacity	Dependability	Generosity	Possibility	Validity
Civility	Diversity	Humility	Purity	Vitality

9

A. Select four words from the above chart and create a question for your partner. Remember to start your question with a question word (Who, What, Where, When, Why, How, Is, Are, Do, Did, Does, etc.). You also want to end each question with a question mark (?). Underline each vocabulary word.

1. ____________________
2. ____________________
3. ____________________
4. ____________________

B. Take turns asking and answering questions with your partner. Ask your instructor to give you feedback on your questions to check your English grammar.

Discussing Quotations

In your small groups, take turns reading these quotations out loud and discuss them. Do you agree with the quotation? Disagree? Why? Mark your opinion. Afterwards, pick a favorite quotation. Remember to give a reason or an example.

1. **"The secret of health for both mind and body is not to mourn for the past, not to worry about the future, not to anticipate troubles, but to live in the present moment wisely and earnestly."**
—Siddhartha Guatama (563–483 B.C.), Buddha, spiritual leader ☐ **Agree** ☐ **Disagree**

2. **"The first duty of a physician is that he should do the sick no harm."**
—Hippocrates (460–380 B.C.), ancient Greek physician ☐ **Agree** ☐ **Disagree**

3. **"It is part of the cure to wish to be cured."**
—Seneca the Younger (4 B.C.–65 A.D.), Roman philosopher/statesmen ☐ **Agree** ☐ **Disagree**

4. **"Better use medicines at the outset than at the last moment."**
—Publilius Syrus (85–43 B.C.E.), Roman writer ☐ **Agree** ☐ **Disagree**

5. **"A sound mind in a sound body is a short, but full description of a happy state in this world."**
—John Locke (1632–1704), English philosopher ☐ **Agree** ☐ **Disagree**

6. **"Early to bed and early to rise makes a man healthy, wealthy, and wise."**
—Benjamin Franklin (1706–1790), American scientist/writer ☐ **Agree** ☐ **Disagree**

7. **"Be careful about reading a health book. You may die of a misprint."**
—Mark Twain (1835–1910), American writer ☐ **Agree** ☐ **Disagree**

8. **"You can't ignore the importance of a good digestion. The joy of life...depends on a sound stomach."**
—Joseph Conrad (1857–1924), Polish-born English author ☐ **Agree** ☐ **Disagree**

9. **"The only way to keep your health is to eat what you don't want, drink what you don't like, and do what you'd rather not."**
—Mark Twain (1835–1910), American humorist ☐ **Agree** ☐ **Disagree**

10. **"Notice the difference between what happens when a man says to himself, I have failed three times,' and what happens when he says, 'I'm a failure.'"**
—S.I. Hayakawa (1906-1992), Japanese-American linguist /U.S. Senator ☐ **Agree** ☐ **Disagree**

Discussion: Which was your favorite quote? Why?

____

____

____

The Conversation Continues

Let's continue to explore topics related to being and staying healthy with one or two classmates. Use complete sentences to respond.

1. Do you exercise regularly? What are your favorite exercises?
2. Do you think you have a healthy lifestyle?
3. Do you eat quickly? Do you eat spicy foods? What else can cause stomach aches?
4. Do you find yourself worrying a lot? What problems worry you?
5. What are the advantages or disadvantages of modern medicine?
6. What are the advantages or disadvantages of traditional medicine?
7. Do you think Americans are overweight? Underweight? Why?
8. Why do you think so many people are living longer today than 100 years ago?
9. Do you restrict your diet for health reasons? How? Why?
10. How has medicine improved over the last 100 years? Ten years?
11. What are some positive health trends?
12. Why do you think so many people are living longer today than 100 years ago?
13. Do you restrict your diet for health reasons? How? Why?
14. How has medicine improved over the last 100 years? Ten years?
15. What are some positive health trends?

Billy Pham | www.billypham.com

Pronunciation Corner

/s/ vs. /sh/

Vietnamese	English
x "xuân"	s "see"
s "sách"	sh "she"

/S/ and /sh/ sounds are perhaps the most frequently confused sounds for Vietnamese learners of English. This pronunciation pattern is because there is only one "in-between" sound in Vietnamese, especially if you have a southern dialect. For native English speakers, though, /s/ and /sh/ are two clearly distinct sounds. The /s/ sound is made by pressing your teeth together and blowing air through the front teeth only. The /sh/ sound is made by pressing the teeth together and blowing air through all sides of the teeth.

As mentioned above, the problem with /s/ and /sh/ is usually not the ability to make the sound, but choosing the right one when speaking. Therefore, we need to pay careful attention to the vowels that follow the sound. A fun American game involves trying to pronounce the following expression: "She sells seashells by the seashore." Note: Many native speakers find this hard too!

Group work: Minimal Bingo

Choose one person to call out random words from the board. When a student has gotten five consecutive choices, say "Bingo." Check against the real answers to make sure the student did not mishear any of the words spoken. The winner gets to call out the next set of words, and the bingo game can continue.

B	I	N	G	O
sea	suit	gas	sore	sip
sheet	leash	she	clash	sign
sip	mesh	★	sell	shore
shine	gash	sue	lease	mess
class	shell	shoot	shoe	seat

Culture Corner

American Laws

There are many laws and rules in America. The United States Constitution says the nation will form an "ever more perfect union." Laws – city, state, or federal - are designed to meet this goal. New laws are usually made when people feel that too many bad things have happened that could be prevented. Sometimes people feel that too many accidents have taken place; sometimes people feel they were mistreated; and sometimes people feel that too many rules are confusing. Legislators – at the city, state, and federal – continually meet and often change laws. By the way, the United States has the most lawyers and the most people in jail in the world.

Billy Pham | www.billypham.com

The legal age to marry in the United States = 16 years old*

Photographer | Tung Phan

The legal age to drive in the United States = 16 years old

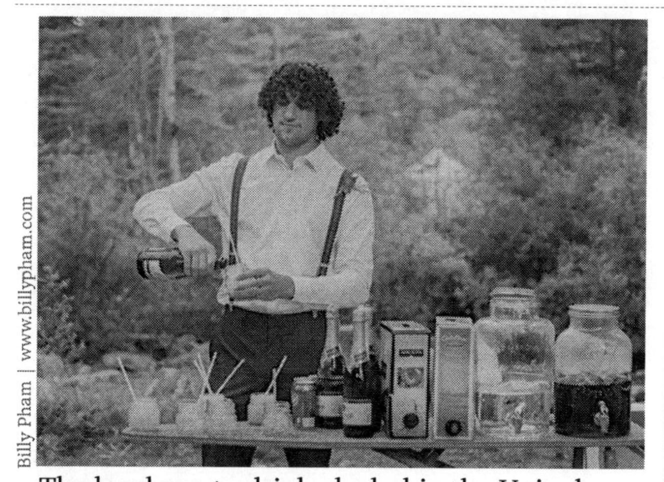
Billy Pham | www.billypham.com

The legal age to drink alcohol in the United States = 21 years old

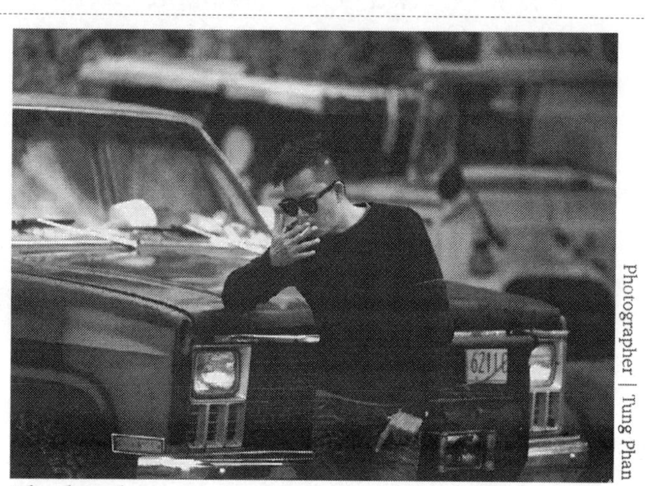
Photographer | Tung Phan

The legal age to smoke in the United States = 18 years old

Activity: True or False?

With a partner, read the laws below. For each law, write T (true) if the law exists or F (false) if the law doesn't exist in somewhere in the U.S. Then discuss why such a law was perhaps created.

___ **1.** It is illegal for a driver to be blindfolded while operating a vehicle.
___ **2.** It is illegal to walk around the city with a bow and arrows.
___ **3.** It is illegal for grocery stores to give plastic bags to its customers.
___ **4.** It is illegal to ride your bicycle over 45 miles per hour.
___ **5.** It is illegal to live on your boat for more than 30 days a year.
___ **6.** It is illegal to have a billboard of any kind.
___ **7.** It is illegal to have a fake boxing contest.
___ **8.** It is illegal to walk around on Saturday with an ice cream in your hand.
___ **9.** It is illegal to sell your skin or eye.
___ **10.** It is illegal to use an x-ray to find your shoe size.

* Individual states determine the laws for marriage, driving, smoking and drinking, but these are the most common ages. The federal government, however, sometimes "encourages" recommended state laws by linking federal funds to specific ages. For instance, states lose federal highway funds if the legal age to drink alcohol is below 21.

Search & Share

Reducing Stress and Increasing Happiness

Student Name:____________________ Date: ____________________

We live in stressful times. How can we reduce our stress? How can we increase our happiness?

A. Take the following five-minute online quiz: "True Happiness Compass."

http://apps.bluezones.com/happiness

Answer the questions, read your evaluation, and be prepared to discuss stress management tips with your classmates.

1. What did you think of the quiz? How many questions were asked?
2. Can you recall two of the questions from the quiz?
3. How would you rate the online quiz, on a scale of 1–5, with five being the highest? Why?

9

B. Find a recent article about how to cope with stress and increase happiness.

Title:____________________ Publication/Website:____________________

Author:____________________ Publication Date: ____________________

1. What's the main idea?
2. How many sources were quoted?
3. How reliable were the sources quoted? Why?
4. What was the strongest part of the article? Why?
5. How would you rate the article on a scale of 1–5, with five being the highest? Why?

"For fast acting relief, try slowing down."
—Lilly Tomlin (1939-), American comedian

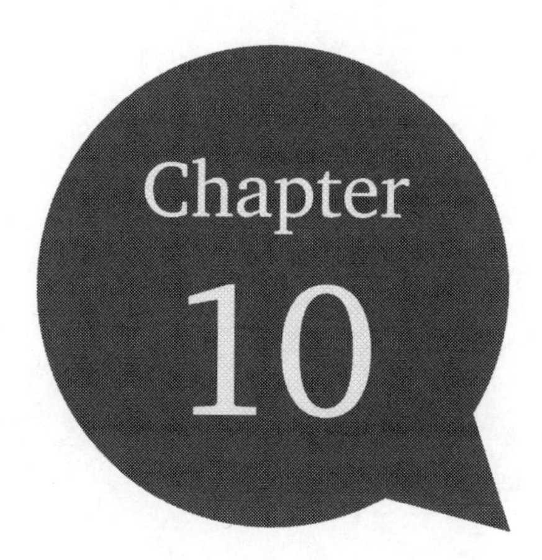

Defining Friendship

"True friends are never apart. Maybe in distance, but never in heart."
–Helen Keller (1880-1968), American author, political activist, and lecturer

Getting Started

How special is your friend?

Billy Pham | www.billypham.com

Directions:
List characteristics that you look for in a friend. After a few minutes, compare your list to your partner. If your partner and you have written down a similar characteristic, cross out that characteristic from both of your list. The person with the most characteristics left wins.

My Friend:

____

____

____

____

____

____

____

____

____

10

Sharing Experiences

Sometimes it is easier to talk the talk than walk the walk when it comes to staying healthy. Interview your partner and exchange health tips.

Billy Pham | www.billypham.com

1. Did you have a best friend when you were a child? Who was it?
2. What did you do together? Can you describe your best friend?
3. Who was your best friend when you were in high school? What did you do together?
4. Are you still friends with the best friends of your youth?
5. Why do best friends sometimes drift apart?
6. What are some tips for keeping a friendship strong?
7. Who is your best friend now? How did you meet your best friend?
8. What activities do you do with your best friend? What makes this friendship special?
9. What do you and your best friend have in common?
10. How are you and your best friend different?
11. In your opinion, are there rules for a friendship? What are they?
12. Do you think you are a good friend to others? In what ways?
13. Do you think friends should loan each other money? Why or why not?
14. What do you like to do with your friends? Where do you like to go?
15. Which of your friends would make good roommates? Why?

On Your Own

Write a letter, by hand or on a computer, to a friend that you have not communicated with recently. What have you been doing since you saw each other? Feel free to include photos, etc. You can share it with your group.

Word List

10

Which words do you already know? Underline them, and circle the words you are unsure about. Then review your answers with a partner.

Noun	Verb	Adjective
crisis /khrai.sịs/	*assist /ờ.sís/	dependable /đì.pen.đa.bồ/
***bond** **/bonđ/**	betray /bì.trê/	supportive /sờ.pó.địv/
roommate /rum.mâyt/	depend /đì.penđ/	
support **/sờ.pót/**	drift /jípht/	
*symbol /sim.bồ/	***bond** **/bonđ/**	

symptom /xim.tầm/	**support** **/sờ.pót/**	
remedy **/re.me.đì/**	*rely /rì.lai/	

*Indicates words on the Academic Word List. See p.204 for all AWL words used in this book.

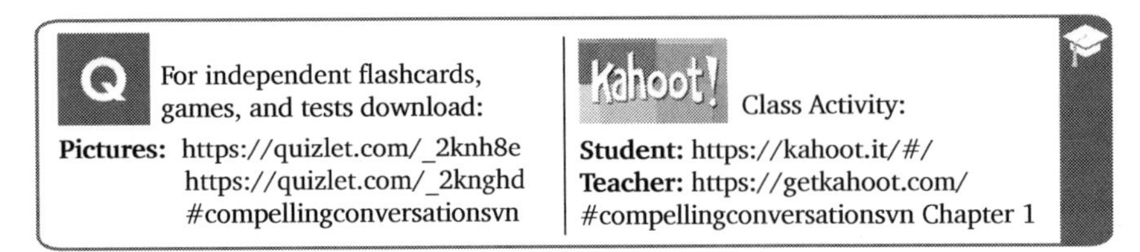

Expanding Vocabulary

Look at the definitions and example sentences below. Do the definitions match what you and your partner expected in the Word List? If not, what is different?

assist [verb]: to help.

> **Ex:** My best friend **assisted** me in cleaning up.

betray [verb]: to violate a trust; to harm or be disloyal.

> **Ex:** I told Kim my secret because I knew she wouldn't **betray** me.

crisis [noun]: an emergency situation; a critical time which requires decisive action.

> **Ex:** The economic **crisis** caused many workers to lose their jobs.

depend [verb]: to count on someone for support or to fulfill a task.

> **Ex:** Children **depend** on their parents for love, protection, and financial support.

dependable [adjective]: loyal, reliable.

> **Ex:** She is **dependable**; you can count on her help during this difficult time.

drift apart [verb]: to slowly separate; to grow distant.

> **Ex:** They were friends for years, but they began to **drift apart** when he moved away for work.

bond [verb]: to tie, to connect.
[noun]: ties, connections.

> Ex: We **bonded** over coffee, conversation, and heartbreak.
> Our school memories are our enduring **bond.**

rely [verb]: to confidently depend on something or someone.

> Ex: You can always **rely** on Xuân Yến for emotional support; she helped me through a bad break-up.

roommate [noun]: someone you live with; a person who shares a house or bedroom with you.

> Ex: I kept the same **roommate** each year I was in college.

support [verb]: to give help, to assist, to recommend, to make stronger.
[noun]: help, assistance, recommendation.

> Ex: She **supported** her best friend during a very hard time.
> The **support** she received from her classmates helped her overcome her fears.

supportive [adjective]: helpful; encouraging.

> Ex: My mother is very **supportive** of my plans to get a graduate degree, but my uncle would prefer I work in his company.

symbol [noun]: an item that embodies an idea or concept; a written character or image that represents a word or phrase.

> Ex: Red roses are considered a **symbol** of romantic love.

? Asking Questions with New Vocabulary Words

A. Select five vocabulary words in this chapter and write a question for each word. Remember to start your question with a question word (Who, What, Where, When, Why, How, Is, Are, Do, Did, Does, etc.). End each question with a question mark (?). Underline each vocabulary word.

Example: *How do your friends <u>support</u> you?*

1. ______________________________
2. ______________________________
3. ______________________________
4. ______________________________
5. ______________________________

B. Take turns asking and answering questions with your partner or group members. Ask your instructor to give you feedback to check your English grammar.

Remember

- Be active
- Be encouraging
- Show understanding

Paraphrasing Proverbs

Read the following proverbs and discuss them with your partner. Write what you think they mean in the spaces provided. Circle your favorites. Explain your choices.

Vietnamese:

Fish will spoil without salt. Children will spoil if they don't listen to their parents.
"Cá không ăn muối cá ươn. Con cưỡng cha mẹ tram đường con hư."
Meaning: ____________________

If you eat the fruit, you have to think about the one who grows the tree.
"Ăn quả nhớ kẻ trồng cây."
Meaning: ____________________

One worm can spoil a whole pot of soup."
"Con sâu làm rầu nồi canh."
Meaning: ____________________

International:

When the character of a man is not clear to you, look at his friends. —Japanese
Meaning: ____________________

Do not protect yourself by a fence, but rather by your friends. —Czech
Meaning: ____________________

Lend money to a good friend, and you will lose the money as well as your friend. —Korean
Meaning: ____________________

Fate chooses your relatives; you choose your friends. —French
Meaning: ____________________

Your best friend is yourself. —American
Meaning: ____________________

Building Words

Adding the Old English Suffix "-ful"

Suffix	Meaning	Example
-ful	full	The word "beauti**ful**" means full of beauty. Likewise, the word "thank**ful**" means full of thanks.

Noah Webster (1758-1843), the creator of the first American dictionary, changed this suffix from "-full" to "-ful" because he thought it was simpler and easier to spell. Webster also wanted his young country, the United States, to develop a distinct form of American English rather than just copying British English. What kind of American English dictionary do you own? Does it have the name Webster in it? Now you know why!

Complete the chart below. For the last two rows, add new root words.

Base	Suffix	New Word
beauty	**-ful**	*beautiful*
care	**-ful**	
cheer	**-ful**	
color	**-ful**	
doubt	**-ful**	
faith	**-ful**	
fear	**-ful**	
help	**-ful**	
tear	**-ful**	
use	**-ful**	
	-ful	
	-ful	

10

A. Select four words from the above chart and create a question for your partner. Remember to start your question with a question word (Who, What, Where, When, Why, How, Is, Are, Do, Did, Does, etc.). You also want to end each question with a question mark (?). Underline each vocabulary word.

1. ______________________________
2. ______________________________
3. ______________________________
4. ______________________________

B. Take turns asking and answering questions with your partner. Ask your instructor to give you feedback to check your English grammar.

On Your Own

Finish the sentence:
A true friend always…
A true friend never…
Discuss your sentences with your partner.

Discussing Quotations

In your small groups, take turns reading these quotations out loud and discuss them. Do you agree with the quotation? Disagree? Why? Mark your opinion. Afterwards, pick a favorite quotation. Remember to give a reason or an example.

1. **"Without friends no one would choose to live, though he had all other goods."**
—Aristotle (384–322 B.C.E.), Greek philosopher ☐ **Agree** ☐ **Disagree**

2. **"Have no friends not equal to yourself."**
—Confucius (551–479 B.C.E.), Chinese philosopher ☐ **Agree** ☐ **Disagree**

3. **"The shifts of Fortune test the reliability of friends."**
—Cicero (106–43 B.C.E.), Roman statesman ☐ **Agree** ☐ **Disagree**

4. **"It is more shameful to distrust our friends than to be deceived by them."**
—Francois de La Rochefoucauld (1613–1680), French philosopher ☐ **Agree** ☐ **Disagree**

5. **"Friendship is the finest balm for the pangs of despised love."**
— Jane Austen (1775 – 1817), English novelist ☐ **Agree** ☐ **Disagree**

6. **"It is easier to forgive an enemy than to forgive a friend."**
—William Blake (1757–1827), English poet ☐ **Agree** ☐ **Disagree**

8. **"Animals are such agreeable friends; they ask no questions, they pass no criticisms."**
—George Eliot/Mary Ann Evans (1819–1880), English novelist ☐**Agree** ☐**Disagree**

9. **"Don't walk behind me, I may not lead. Don't walk in front of me, I may not follow. Just walk beside me and be my friend."**
—Albert Camus (1913–1960), French author/journalist, Nobel Prize winner (1957) ☐**Agree** ☐**Disagree**

10. **"A true friend is the most precious of possessions, and the one we take least thought about acquiring."**
—Francois de La Rochefoucauld (1613-1680), French philosopher ☐**Agree** ☐**Disagree**

Discussion: Which was your favorite quote? Why?

____

____

____

The Conversation Continues

10

Let's continue to explore topics related to friendship with one or two classmates. Use complete sentences to respond.

Billy Pham | www.billypham.com

1. Have you ever lived with a roommate? What makes a good roommate?
2. How do you meet new friends? What do you look for in new friends?
3. How do you keep in touch with friends? Why do some friendships survive even when friends live far away?

4. How can you form strong bonds with classmates?
5. Do you think that people of the opposite sex can be friends? Why?
6. Have you ever felt betrayed by a friend? How did you react?
7. Do you think it is fair to judge people by their friends? Why?
8. Do you have a close circle of friends? What unites you?
9. Can one be friends with one's parents? Why or why not?
10. How do you know when someone is a friend?
11. Do you think the definition of friend has changed over time? How?
12. There is a saying "To have a good friend, you need to be a good friend." How can you be a good friend?
13. Where is a good place to make new friends?
14. What is the purpose of having a friend?
15. What do you usually do with your friends?

Pronunciation Corner

/f/ vs. /p/

The /p/ is difficult for Vietnamese learners of English because it does not exist in the Vietnamese language. To make the /p/sound, bring both lips together and then release air in an explosive manner. To practice, hold a piece of paper in front of your mouth. Make the /p/ sound and then watch the paper move as a result of the air released while making the sound. If your paper does not move, you are making the incorrect sound.

Vietnamese	English
p "phở"	f "fan"
n/a	p "pen"

Pair work: Silent Speaking

Look at the list of words below. Practice silently "saying" the words without using your voice and making a sound. Your partner should be able to look at your mouth and guess if you are trying to use /f/ or /p/.

/f/	/p/
face	pace
fat	pat

foot	**p**ut
fan	**p**an
fast	**p**ast
fool	**p**ool
fail	**p**ail
lau**gh**	la**p**
wife	wi**p**e
cli**ff**	cli**p**
lea**f**	lea**p**
bee**f**	bee**p**

Culture Corner

Friendships

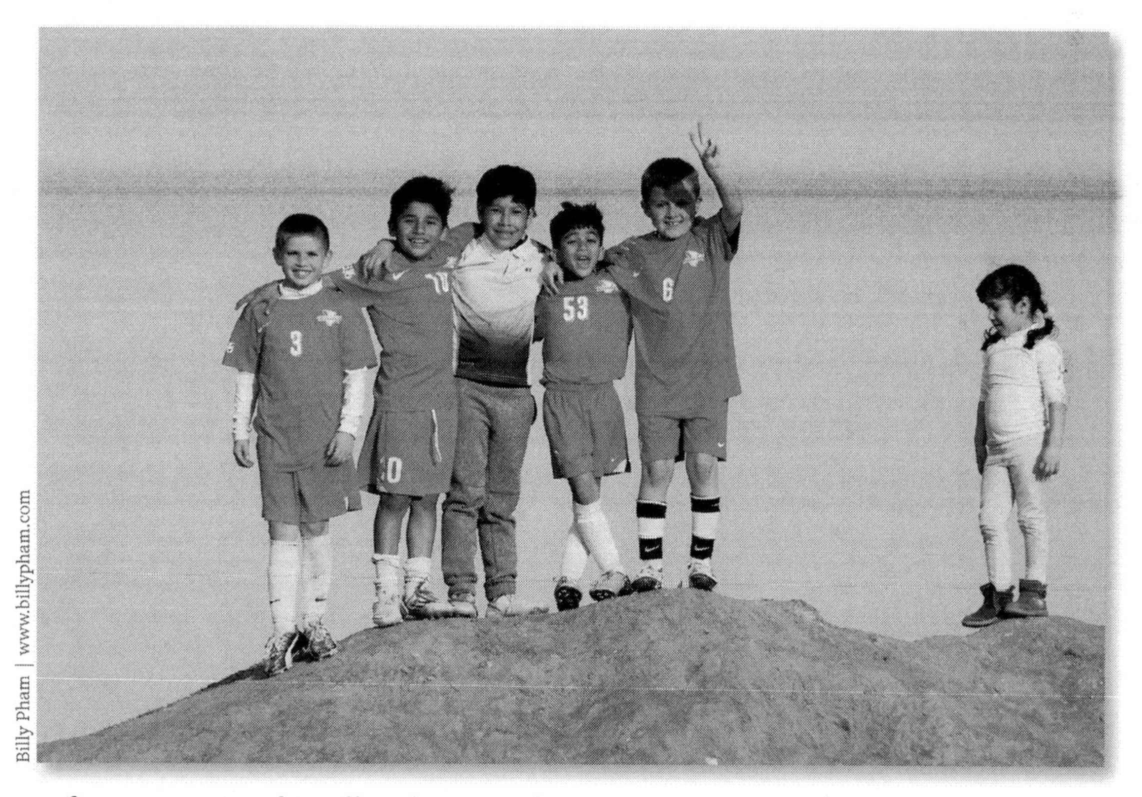

Billy Pham | www.billypham.com

Americans often seem very friendly when you first meet them. This friendliness does not always mean that the person is looking for a deeper relationship. Many Americans are pleasant and professional, but indirect and hide their true emotions. Being polite is important in American culture. Sometimes this can be confusing to foreigners. Americans will sometimes act nice to you even if they do not wish to pursue a deeper friendship.

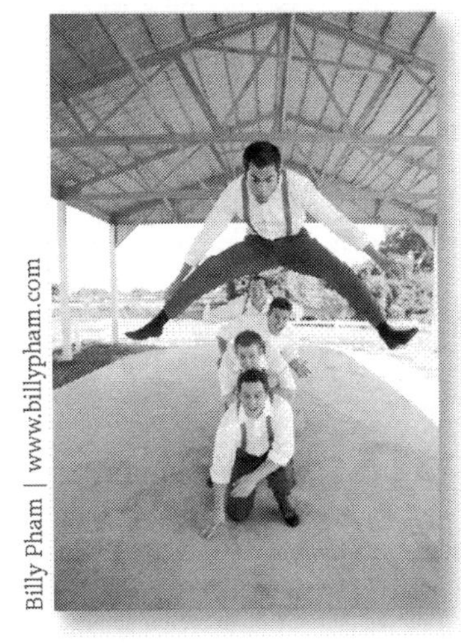

Categories of Friends

Friendships between Americans tend to be shorter and less demanding than in some more traditional societies. Perhaps because Americans live in a competitive and fast-paced society, they tend to see friendships as more situation-based. As a result, friendships are specified into categories depending on their relationship status:

1. Friends from work
2. Friends from school
3. Friends from church, mosque, or temple
4. Family friends
5. Neighbors

Some Americans avoid mixing these categories of friends too. For example, you may ask somebody from work to go watch a movie, but they may tell you that they already have plans to see it with other friends. It may seem unusual that your colleague did not invite you to join his/her other friends to see the movie, but Americans who may be interested in getting to know you may decline invitations unless the correct "category of friends" is attending. If you express your interest in going out again, you might be invited to another event in which "work friends" are involved. Plus, it is also possible that categories of friends may overlap as time passes.

Friends with the Opposite Sex

It is common for many American women to have male friends that are just friends and vice versa. As a habit, many Americans hug a lot. Therefore, it's not uncommon for American men and women to hug as a greeting or a leave-taking even though they aren't particularly close. Additionally, sometimes American men and women even share a living space without having any sexual relationship. However, when making friends with the opposite sex, it is safest to first meet in a public space (e.g. coffee shop, movie theatre) many times before you ride in a car

Activity: With a partner, discuss the similarities and differences of friendships in the U.S and another country you have lived in or visited.

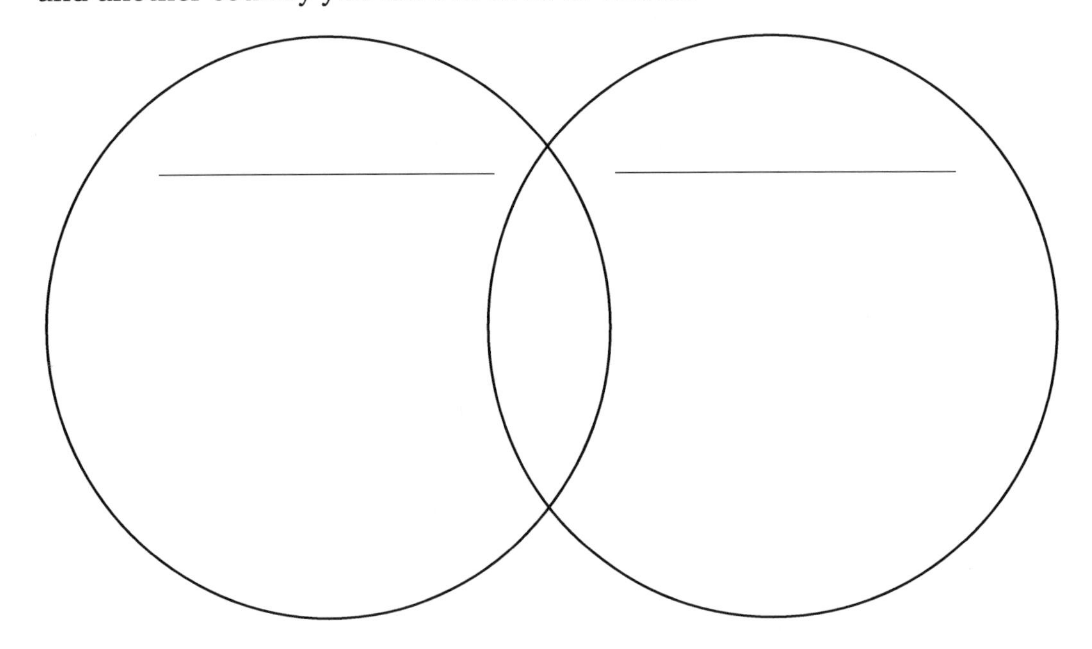

Search & Share

Chatting in Person and Online

Clara Hutzler | www.hellosuitcase.com

Student Name: ______________________

Date: ______________________

Find an article about how friendship has changed since Facebook, Google+, and Twitter have become so popular. Do you think social media changes friendships? How so?

Read the article, print it out, and be prepared to discuss it with classmates.

Title: ______________________ Publication/Website: ______________________

Author: ______________________ Publication Date: ______________________

1. What's the title of the article?
2. What's the main idea?
3. How many sources were quoted?
4. Were there any illustrations? What kind?
5. What did you learn from this article?
6. What was the most interesting part for you? Why?
7. Which do you like better, the way friendships were before social networks or the way things are now? Why?
8. Write five new vocabulary words, idioms, or expressions related to the article.
9. How would you rate the article on a scale of 1–5, with five being the highest? Why?
10. Why did you choose this article to share with your classmates?

10

> **"Have friends. It's a second existence."**
> —Baltasar Gracian (1601–1658), Spanish philosopher

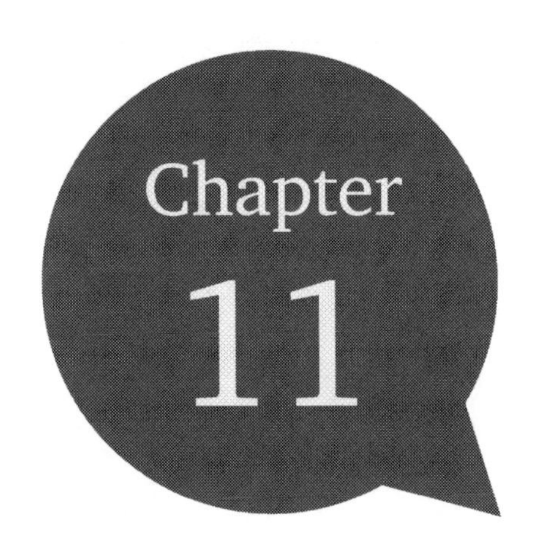

Bitter to Better

> **"A quick temper will make a fool of you soon enough."**
> – Bruce Lee (1940-1973), Hong Kong/American actor and martial artist

Getting Started

Billy Pham | www.billypham.com

Not My Type

Directions:
Mark the following on a scale of 1 to 5 depending on how much you agree or disagree with these rules for personal hygiene. Then add your own rules that have not been stated.

1 = agree
5 = disagree

__1. Women: wear make-up every day.
__2. Brush your teeth after every meal.
__3. Comb or brush your hair every morning.
__4. Change your toothbrush every month.
__5. Men: shave facial hair.
__6. Shower morning and night.
__7. Use perfume or cologne every day.
__8. Wash your hair once a week.
__9. Wash your hands after using the toilet.
__10. Wash your hands before you eat.
__11. ____________________
__12. ____________________
__13. ____________________
__14. ____________________

Sharing Experiences

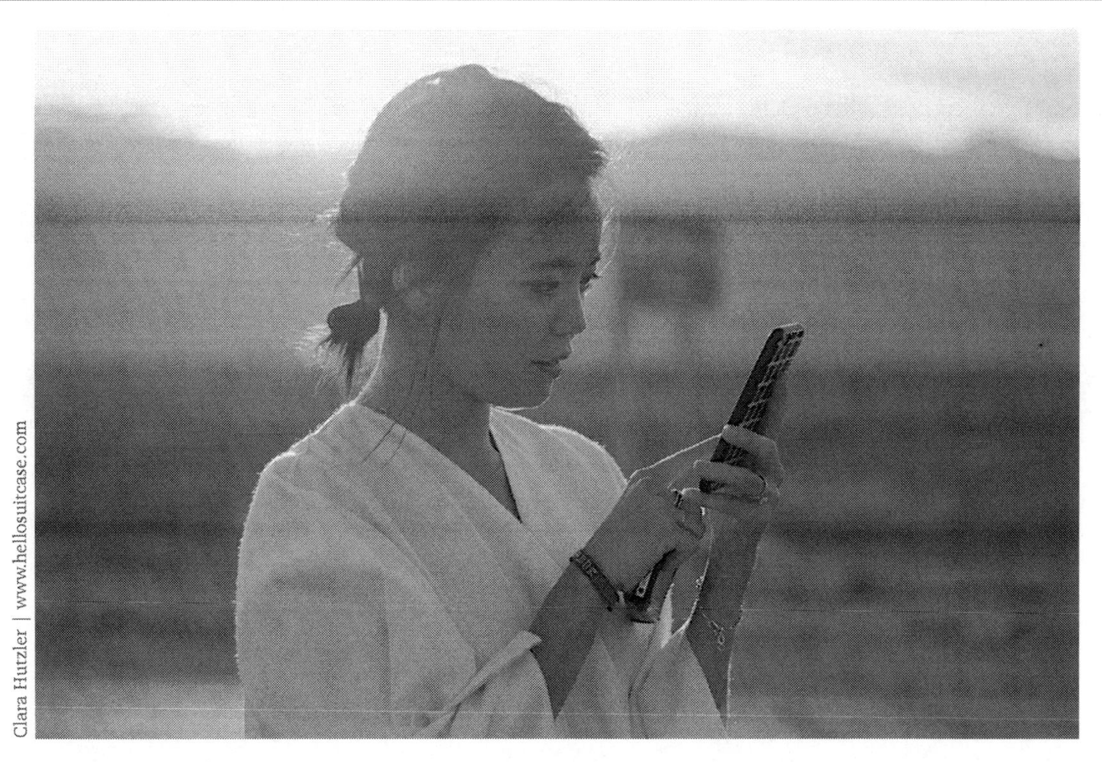
Clara Hutzler | www.hellosuitcase.com

Sometimes things annoy us, and that's okay. Share your complaints and pet peeves with your partner. Talking and sharing our frustrations and complaints can sometimes help us feel better in difficult situations.

1 What annoys you? Do you have any pet peeves at home or at work?

2 What are some of the things people do that you find impolite? Can you give a couple of examples?

3. How can sales people be annoying? Can you give some examples?
4. Have you ever had phone problems? How did you respond? Do technical "glitches" or problems bother you?
5. Do you know many people who share your pet peeves? Which ones?
6. What sounds bother you? What do you feel when you hear them?
7. What are some sounds you find annoying? Burping? Sneezing? Blowing one's nose in public?
8. What are some things you find annoying about the way people talk?
9. What is litter? Have you seen any litterbugs? Where does litter bother you the most? Do you pick it up?
10. What do you consider bad cell phone manners? Why?
11. When, or where, do you most often see people get stressed? Can you give an example?
12. What behavior by a neighbor might be considered annoying?
13. How do you feel about aggressive people? Is there a difference between assertive and aggressive?
14. What is something that people do that you find mean, wrong, or immoral?
15. Is there something else you can't stand? Do you have other pet peeves?

Word List

Which words do you already know? Underline them, and circle the words you are unsure about. Then review your answers with a partner.

Noun	Verb	Adjective
courtesy /khơ.đờ.sì/	annoy /ớ.noi/	impolite /im.pồ.lait/
litter **/lia.đờ/**	bother /bo.đờ/	obnoxious /ậb.no.chịs/
pet peeve /pét.piv/	litter /lia.đờ/	offended /ậb.phen.địt/
profanity /prồ.phen.ny.đì/	mitigate /mê.thi/ghệt/	
*conduct /khẩn.đất/		
*criteria /khrài.thia.rì.à/		

*Indicates words on the Academic Word List. See p.204 for all AWL words used in this book.

For independent flashcards, games, and tests download:

Pictures: https://quizlet.com/_2knpfh
https://quizlet.com/_2knp13
#compellingconversationsvn

Kahoot! Class Activity:

Student: https://kahoot.it/#/
Teacher: https://getkahoot.com/
#compellingconversationsvn Chapter 11

Expanding Vocabulary

Look at the definitions and example sentences below. Do the definitions match what you and your partner expected in the Word List? If not, what is different?

annoy [verb]: to disturb or irritate.

> Ex: Loud traffic **annoys** me when I'm trying to sleep at night.

bother [verb]: to annoy, to disrupt or disturb; to make one feel bad.

> Ex: Please don't **bother** me while I'm talking on the phone.

conduct [noun] a person's behavior depending on the situation.

> Ex: Gia Uy always **conducted** himself with respect when speaking with others.

courtesy [noun]: a kind or polite act; politeness.

> Ex: It is common **courtesy** to hold a door open for others.

criteria [noun] a standard to be met.

> Ex: This paper is well written, but doesn't meet the **criteria** of the assignment.

11

impolite [adjective]: poor behavior, rude.

> Ex: It's **impolite** to spit on the floor.

litter [noun]: trash that can be seen on the street; garbage on the ground; a number of dogs or cats born at the same time to the same mother.

> Ex: **Litter** has become a major problem in some large cities without enough public trashcans.
> My dog gave birth to a **litter** of six puppies.

mitigate [verb]: to reduce a problem, to lessen the negative impact of something.

> **Ex:** In order to **mitigate** the impact of the new apartment complex on local streets, the city ordered the developer to create 100 new parking spaces.

obnoxious [adjective]: extremely annoying; bothersome.

> **Ex:** It's **obnoxious** to throw leftover food on the street like a litterbug.

offended [adjective]: feeling upset or insulted.

> **Ex:** I feel **offended** when you use ugly, vulgar, and rude words to insult me.

pet peeve [noun]: something which annoys or irritates a person.

> **Ex:** My biggest **pet peeve** is when my neighbors watch TV loudly late at night while I'm trying to sleep.

profanity [noun]: a filthy word; offensive language.

> **Ex:** Should a parent punish a child who uses **profanity** in public?

? Asking Questions with New Vocabulary Words

A. Select five vocabulary words in this chapter and write a question for each word. Remember to start your question with a question word (Who, What, Where, When, Why, How, Is, Are, Do, Did, Does, etc.). You also want to end each question with a question mark (?). Underline each vocabulary word.

Example: *Who is the most impolite person you know?*

1. ______________________________
2. ______________________________
3. ______________________________
4. ______________________________
5. ______________________________

B. Take turns asking and answering questions with your partner or group members. Ask your instructor to give you feedback on your questions to check your English grammar.

Paraphrasing Proverbs

Read the following proverbs and discuss them with your partner. Write what you think they mean in the spaces provided. Circle your favorites. Explain your choices.

Vietnamese:

Water drops wear the stone.
"Nước chảy đá mòn."
Meaning: ______

Lost time can't be found.
"Thời giờ đã mất thì không tìm lại được."
Meaning: ______

No fire. No smoke.
"Không có lửa sao có khói."
Meaning: ______

International:

Recite "patience" three times and it will spare you a murder. —Korean
Meaning: ______

Hatred is as blind as love. —Irish proverb
Meaning: ______

Control yourself: remember anger is only one letter short of danger. —American high school poster
Meaning: ______

Love makes a good eye squint. —English
Meaning: ______

The reputation of a thousand years may be determined by the conduct of one hour. —Japanese
Meaning: ______

Remember

- be clear
- be honest
- be fair

Adding the Latin Prefix "mis-"

The common prefix "mis" means wrong or wrongly. The word misunderstand, for instance, means to wrongly understand something. For instance, "Are these instructions clear? Do you understand? Or is there some misunderstanding that we can clarify?"

Prefix	Meaning	Example
mis-	wrong/wrongly bad or ill	The word "**mis**place" means to put something in the wrong place. A "**mis**print" is a bad print.

Complete the chart. Do the following mean "inside" or "not?"

Prefix	Base	New Word
mis-	understand	*misunderstand*
mis-	behave	
mis-	calculate	
mis-	deed	
mis-	perception	
mis-	print	
mis-	pronounce	
mis-	translate	
mis-	treat	
mis-	label	
mis-		
mis-		

11

A. Select four words from the above chart and create a question for your partner. Remember to start your question with a question word (Who, What, Where, When, Why, How, Is, Are, Do, Did, Does, etc.). End each question with a question mark (?). Underline each vocabulary word.

1. ______
2. ______
3. ______
4. ______

B. Take turns asking and answering questions with your partner. Ask your instructor to give you feedback on your questions to check your English grammar.

On Your Own

Prepare a one-minute presentation on your biggest pet peeve that you may later give to the class.

____

____

____

____

Discussing Quotations

In your small groups, take turns reading these quotations out loud and discuss them. Do you agree with the quotation? Disagree? Why? Mark your opinion. Afterwards, pick a favorite quotation. Remember to give a reason or an example.

1. **"The test of good manners is to be patient with bad ones."**
   —Solomon ibn Gabriol (1021–1051), Hebrew poet/philosopher ☐ **Agree** ☐ **Disagree**

2. **"Good manners are made up of petty sacrifices."**
   —Ralph Waldo Emerson (1803–1882), American essayist ☐ **Agree** ☐ **Disagree**

3. **"Be polite; write diplomatically; even in a declaration of war, one observes the rules of politeness."**
   —Otto von Bismarck (1815–1898), German statesman ☐ **Agree** ☐ **Disagree**

4. **"Never treat a guest like a member of the family—treat him with courtesy."**
   —Evan Esar (1899–1935), American humoris ☐ **Agree** ☐ **Disagree**

5. **"If you don't have anything nice to say, come sit by me."**
   —Alice Roosevelt Longworth (1884–1980), fashion icon U.S. President Theodore Roosevelt's daughter ☐ **Agree** ☐ **Disagree**

6. **"When you're down and out, something always turns up —usually the noses of your friends."**
   —Orson Welles (1915–1985), American actor/director ☐ **Agree** ☐ **Disagree**

7. **"Those who do not complain are never pitied."**
   —Jane Austen (1775-1819), English novelist ☐ **Agree** ☐ **Disagree**

8. "There are bad manners everywhere, but an aristocracy is bad manners organized."
—Henry James (1843-1916), American writer ☐ **Agree** ☐ **Disagree**

9. "Kindness is the language which the deaf can hear and the blind can see."
—Mark Twain (1835-1910), American writer ☐ **Agree** ☐ **Disagree**

10. "I have the simplest taste. I am always satisfied with the best."
—Oscar Wilde (1854-1900), Irish writer ☐ **Agree** ☐ **Disagree**

Discussion: Which was your favorite quote? Why?

____

____

____

The Conversation Continues

Let's continue to explore topics related to pet peeves with one or two classmates. Use complete sentences to respond.

Billy Pham | www.billypham.com

1. What table manners or eating styles make you frown or annoy you?
2. When, if ever, does snoring, sneezing, or coughing bother you?
3. How does a polite child act in public? How might a rude child misbehave?
4. Where do people learn good manners? What are good manners?

5. What's the best way to teach manners to children?
6. Can manners affect your success in life? How?
7. Can you describe a polite boss? A very difficult boss?
8. How can someone annoy you? Has anyone every annoyed you? What did they do? How did you handle the situation?
9. Does foul language or profanity, upset you? When?
10. What is your advice for dealing with difficult, moody, or "toxic" people?
11. Have you seen any changes in what are considered good manners? What are they?
12. What is something that once annoyed you that you have, over time, come to tolerate?
13. What are some manners that no longer exist?
14. What brings out the worst in you?
15. How can people bring out your best side?

Pronunciation Corner

/th/ vs. /t/

Vietnamese learners commonly replace /th/ with /t/ when speaking because /th/ does not exist in Vietnamese. The unvoiced /th/ sound needs to be pronounced by putting your tongue between your teeth (or sticking it out!). Some Vietnamese students find this embarrassing, but remember, this is English. It's ok to look a little silly!

Vietnamese	English
t "tu"	n/a
th "thu"	t "toy"
n/a	th "them"

11

Pair work: Thumbs up, thumbs down.

Student A: Choose any word on the /th/ or /t/ words list below and say it out loud.

Student B: If Student A says a /th/ word, partner B gives the thumbs up sign. If they say a /t/ word, partner B should give the thumbs down sign.

When you get three thumbs up in a row, switch roles.

/th/	/t/
bath	bat
both	boat
thank	tank
booth	boot
faith	fate
Ruth	root
math	mat
wrath	rat
path	pat
three	tree
thin	tin
tenth	tent
thick	tick
teeth	teat

Culture Corner

Personal Hygiene

Billy Pham | www.billypham.com

Have you noticed how many items in American stores are scented? American consumers buy hand soaps, detergents, lotions, candles, markers and even stickers that are scented. The reason is that many Americans remain very sensitive to smells, especially natural body odors and bad breath.

However, although most Americans prefer not to be near people with strong natural body odors, it is not common practice to use extremely large amounts of perfume or cologne. Americans consider perfume to be a pleasant smell only if it is subtle and can be smelled when people are very close to them. As a matter of fact, some hospitals discourage perfume or cologne at work or when visiting in-home patients because the scents may directly affect the health of patients who have asthma or other illnesses.

As a result, maintaining a natural personal hygiene is the preferred method. Some American practices include:

Billy Pham | www.billypham.com

1. brush their teeth every morning and evening
2. change clothes every day
3. shower every day
4. use deodorant or antiperspirant to prevent body odor
5. wash their hair at least several times a week

Activity: With a partner, share five other practices that make a positive, healthy impression?

____

____

____

____

____

11

"Wisdom is not a product of schooling but of the lifelong attempt to acquire it."
—Albert Einstein (1879-1955), American scientist

Customer Complaints and Practicing Prepositions

Activity 1:

We often need to use proper English to solve problems at work. Work with your conversation partner and find the right preposition to fill in the missing blank. Take turns reading sentences and determine which sentences are replies to complaints. The prepositions are grouped together for clarity. After filling in each group determine whether the speaker is making a complaint or responding to a complaint.

To
- I'm writing _______ complain about your customer service helpline.
- I'm calling _______ make a complaint.
- I wish _______ make an inquiry about something on my monthly bill.
- I've been trying _______ get through to you for two weeks.
- The order was delivered _______ the wrong branch.
- I'm sorry that I didn't get back _______ you sooner.
- The delay wasn't our fault. It was due _______ the bad weather.

On
- The delivery arrived _______ the wrong day.
- If you can't deliver _______ time, we'll have to contact other suppliers.
- I would like to apologize _______ behalf of (name of company) for any inconvenience.

For
- Please accept our apologies _______ the inconvenience.
- We would like to offer you a discount on your next order to make up _______ our mistake.
- Thank you _______ bringing this matter to my attention.
- I'm sorry _______ sending the documents to the wrong address.
- Who signed _______the delivery?

11

Of
- Please find a list _______ the missing items.
- There were a number _______ mistakes on the invoice.
- Several _______ our delivery vehicles are out of service.
- We were closed for a number _______ days due to the floods.

About
- I'm sorry. I'm calling to complain _______ your payment system.
- I'm calling _______ my order. It isn't here yet.
- I'd like to learn _______ your refund policy.

Under

- The product is no longer _______ warranty.
- We found your order _______ someone else's name.
- Would you please look _______ the counter to see if there are more?
- I'd like to see the yellow shirt_______ the blue one.

With

- We had some problems _______ the instruction booklet.
- _______ reference to your December 1st email, it seems that an error has been made.
- We are not satisfied _______ the quality of the products.
- I have checked _______ the staff involved, and they claim they were not responsible.

In

- _______ fact, we had already paid the full bill the previous week.
- We will do our best to ensure that such mistakes do not occur again _______ the future.
- Are you sure it was included _______ the shipment?
- We can loan you a free rental car _______ a few days.

Into

- We will look _______ it right away and get back to you as soon as we can.
- I would be grateful if you could look _______ the matter.

At

- I believe your misleading salesman is _______ fault.
- Would you please look _______ the bill I received?
- Our records show the package was received ___ your address.

By

- We strongly believe that the mistake was made _______ your company.
- We will correct the mistake _______ noon today.
- The part will be replaced _______ the manufacturer.

11

Activity 2:

Write three consumer complaints with a preposition.

1. ______________________________
2. ______________________________
3. ______________________________

Write three responses to consumer complaints with prepositions.

1. ______________________________
2. ______________________________
3. ______________________________

Search & Share

Give a Product Review

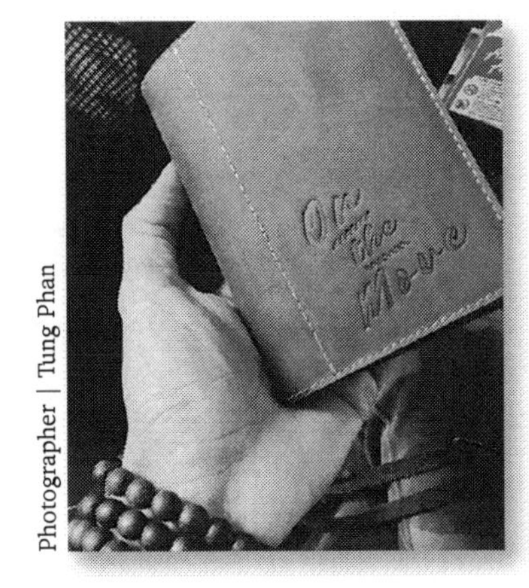

Photographer | Tung Phan

Student Name: ____________________

Date: ____________________

Product reviews are increasingly popular, and you can find many places to share reviews. For your next class, pick a consumer product to review. Do some research online about the product. Find at least two sources of information. Then fill in this worksheet, and create a product review to share with your classmates.

Product: ____________________ Company: ____________________

Source: ____________________ Date: ____________________

1. Do you own the product?

2. What is the purpose of the product?

3. Who is the target audience for this product? Who usually uses it?

4. How is the product used?

5. What does the product cost?

6. What competitors does the product have?

7. Are there some possible dangers or misuses of the product?

8. What did you learn during your research about this product?

9. Do you recommend this product for your classmates? Why?

10. How do you rate the product on a scale of 1–5, with 5 being the highest? Why?

11

> **"The customer is always right."**
> —American proverb

Chapter 12 Exploring Cities

"**What is the city but the people?**"
—William Shakespeare (1564-1616), English playwright

Duong Trinh | @minhduongtrinh94

Getting Started

Survivor in a New City

Photographer | Tung Phan

Directions:
With a partner, make a list of 10 items that you would bring if you were moving alone to a new city in another country. What are the things that you most treasure? What are the things that you need to survive and thrive in a foreign city?

- ______________________________
- ______________________________
- ______________________________
- ______________________________
- ______________________________
- ______________________________
- ______________________________
- ______________________________
- ______________________________
- ______________________________

Sharing Experiences

Billy Pham | www.billypham.com

Cities can be confusing, exciting, and fast-paced. Some people love living in cities; and some people prefer living in the countryside. Share your experiences and feelings about American and Vietnamese cities with your partner.

1. Were you born in a city or the countryside? How far is your birth place from here?
2. What do you like to do in cities? Why?
3. Which Vietnamese cities have you visited?
4. How do people usually get around Vietnamese cities?
5. Can you tell me about a famous district in a Vietnamese city?
6. Have you been to Hà Nội yet? How often?
7. What makes the capital of Vietnam an attractive city?
8. Can you describe some historic places in Hanoi?
9. Which Vietnamese city do you know best? Why?
10. What adjectives describe Hồ Chí Minh City? Why?
11. How has Hồ Chí Minh City (or another Vietnamese city) changed in the last decade?
12. Which Vietnamese cities have important archaeological areas?
13. What other cities have you been to in Vietnam? The United States?
14. Compare two Vietnamese cities. How are they similar? Different?
15. Compare two American cities. How are they similar? Different?

On Your Own

List 10 cities from around the world. For each city, write down two adjectives to describe that city. For example: Huế - beautiful, ancient.

1. ______ 6. ______
2. ______ 7. ______
3. ______ 8. ______
4. ______ 9. ______
5. ______ 10. ______

Word List

Which words do you already know? Underline them, and circle the words you are unsure about. Then review your answers with a partner.

Noun	Verb	Adjective
archeology /o.kỷ.o.lờ.ji/	**commute /khờ.mưut/**	
attraction /ờ.trác.shần/	***fund /phând/**	
capital /khab.bi.đồ/		
hometown /hôm.thaon/		
landmark /lenn.mạk/		
*section /xéc.shần/		
skyscraper /xcai.xrếb.bờ/		
slum /slâm/		
zone /zôn/		
*region /ri.chần/		
***fund /phând/**		
commute /khờ.mưut/		

12

*Indicates words on the Academic Word List. See p.204 for all AWL words used in this book.

Q For independent flashcards, games, and tests download:
Pictures: https://quizlet.com/_2knooc
https://quizlet.com/_2kno8c
#compellingconversationsvn

Class Activity:
Student: https://kahoot.it/#/
Teacher: https://getkahoot.com/
#compellingconversationsvn Chapter 12

Expanding Vocabulary

Look at the definitions and example sentences below. Do the definitions match what you and your partner expected in the Word List? If not, what is different?

archaeology [noun]: the study of historic sites and ancient buildings.

> Ex: **Archaeology** helped make Huế a World Heritage Site, where archaeologists can study the city's many ancient buildings, beautiful temples, and royal palaces.

attraction [noun]: a natural force which acts to bring people or things together.

> Ex: Hạ Long Bay has become Vietnam's greatest tourist **attraction**.

capital [noun]: a city that is the seat of government in a country or state; money invested and used to create more wealth.

> Ex: Hà Nội is the charming **capital** of Vietnam.
> Adequate **capital** makes opening a new business much easier.

commute [noun]: the time or path of travel to your job from your home and back every day.
[verb]: to travel regularly to and from a destination.

> Ex: My **commute** to campus is only 20 minutes by motorbike, but it used to take much longer when I rode my bicycle.
> I **commute** to school by motorbike.

12

fund [noun] an available amount of money, or money with a designated purpose.
[verb]: to provide money for a purpose.

> Ex: The university alumni **fund** provides grants to fund research the history of the small liberal arts college.

hometown [noun]: the city where a person was born.

> Ex: Đà Nẵng is my **hometown**, but I have lived in Hồ Chí Minh City for three years.

landmark [noun]: a place of historical or cultural importance; a significant event or idea.

> **Ex:** The Eiffel Tower in Paris, France and the Statue of Liberty in New York City are famous **landmarks** recognized around the world.

region [noun]: an area of a country that is geographically or culturally distinct from the others.

> **Ex:** I'm visiting relatives in the Northeastern **region** of the country.

section [noun]: area, part, or neighborhood.

> **Ex:** The mayor announced several projects to improve the poor **sections** of the city.

skyscraper [noun]: a high rise building in a city; a tall office tower.

> **Ex:** The tallest **skyscraper** in the world is in Dubai, a modern city in the Middle East.

slum [noun]: the poor, overcrowded section of a city.

> **Ex:** The fashionable neighborhood used to be a **slum**, but it has been rebuilt over time by new families living in modern apartments.

zone [noun]: a technique of land-use planning; laws that restrict how property can be used in a specific area.

> **Ex:** The new **zoning** laws will widen streets, ban street parking, and reduce traffic jams on the old, narrow streets.

? Asking Questions with New Vocabulary Words

12

A. Select five vocabulary words in this chapter and write a question for each word. Remember to start your question with a question word (Who, What, Where, When, Why, How, Is, Are, Do, Did, Does, etc.). You also want to end each question with a question mark (?). Underline each vocabulary word.

Example: *What are some local landmarks?*

1. ____________________
2. ____________________
3. ____________________
4. ____________________
5. ____________________

B. Take turns asking and answering questions with your partner or group members. Ask your instructor to give you feedback on your questions to check your English grammar.

Remember

• Be alert • Be careful • Be kind • Be safe

Paraphrasing Proverbs

Read the following proverbs and discuss them with your partner. Write what you think they mean in the spaces provided. Circle your favorites. Explain your choices.

Vietnamese:

Go to know this and that. Staying at home with Mom, when will you know?
"Đi cho biết đó biết đây, ở nhà với mẹ biết ngày nào khôn."
Meaning: ______________________________

Things that have passed, let it pass.
"Việc gì qua rồi hãy cho qua."
Meaning: ______________________________

Money can even buy a fairy.
"Có tiền mua tiên cũng được."
Meaning: ______________________________

International:

Rome wasn't built in a day. —Latin
Meaning: ______________________________

The city for wealth; the country for health. —English
Meaning: ______________________________

A city that sits on a hill can't be hidden. —Greek
Meaning: ______________________________

Go to the country to hear the news of town. —American
Meaning: ______________________________

Good and bad make up a city. —Portuguese
Meaning: ______________________________

The Conversation Continues

Billy Pham | www.billypham.com

Let's continue to explore topics related to exploring cities with one or two classmates. Use complete sentences to respond.

1. What do you expect to find in a modern city? Why?
2. How do you prepare for trips to new cities?
3. While traveling, were you ever afraid? Why?
4. While traveling, were you ever lost? Where were you?
5. Have you ever taken a group tour? When?
6. Do you feel safer in cities or in rural areas? Why?
7. What are some popular tourist destinations in your hometown? Have you been to any of them? Which one would you recommend?
8. What are the benefits of travelling?
9. Has any place surprised you? How was it different from what you expected?
10. Where would you like to travel next? Why? What would you most like to see?
11. Which cities have hosted the Olympics Games? Do you remember when?
12. What are some cities that have hosted World Cup championships?
13. Name some famous landmarks around the world.
14. Do you prefer to travel by train, bus, plane or ship? Why?
15. What is the most beautiful/interesting place you've ever been to? Why?

EXPLORE A NEW CITY!

Select one of the 10 cities that you would like to visit. Find out more about the city. Use the worksheet called "Exploring a Foreign City" at the end of this chapter. Be ready to talk about the city for a few minutes in a group during the next class. Your teacher may call for brave volunteers to present to the class.

Building Words

Adding the Old English Suffix "-less"

What is the opposite of full? The word "empty" might come to mind since we know that an empty tank of gas is the opposite of a full tank of gas. We might also say zero or none. We previously studied the suffix –ful, a short version for full, in words like "careful," "beautiful," and "painful." Now we're look at the other suffix, -less, which is often the opposite and means without. Therefore, the word "painless" – meaning without pain- is the opposite of "painful."

Suffix	Meaning	Example
-less	without	The word "pain**less**" means without pain. We all want our visits to the dentists to be "pain**less**" or without pain.

Complete the chart below by following the example. For the last two rows, add new root words.

Base	Suffix	New Word
care	**-less**	*careless*
cheer	**-less**	
color	**-less**	
doubt	**-less**	
faith	**-less**	
fear	**-less**	
help	**-less**	
tear	**-less**	
use	**-less**	
time	**-less**	
	-less	

12

Asking Questions with New Vocabulary Words

A. Select five vocabulary words in this chapter and write a question for each word. Remember to start your question with a question word (Who, What, Where, When, Why, How, Is, Are, Do, Did, Does, etc.). End each question with a question mark (?). Underline each vocabulary word.

Example: *what is something painless?*

1. ____
2. ____
3. ____
4. ____
5. ____

B. Take turns asking and answering questions with your partner or group members. Ask your instructor to check your English grammar.

Discussing Quotations

In your small groups, take turns reading these quotations out loud and discuss them. Do you agree with the quotation? Disagree? Why? Mark your opinion. Afterwards, pick a favorite quotation. Remember to give a reason or an example.

1. **"It is men who make a city, not walls or ships."**
   —Thucydides (460 BCE – 395 BCE), Greek historian ☐ **Agree** ☐ **Disagree**

2. **"The world is a book and those who do not travel read only one page."**
   —Augustine of Hippo (354-430), Catholic philosopher ☐ **Agree** ☐ **Disagree**

3. **"City life: millions of people being lonesome together."**
   —Henry David Thoreau (1817-1862), American writer ☐ **Agree** ☐ **Disagree**

4. **"What you want is to have a city which everyone can admire as being something finer and more beautiful than he had ever dreamed of before."**
   —James Bryce (1838-1922), American architect ☐ **Agree** ☐ **Disagree**

5. **"Paris is a city of...pleasures where four-fifths of the inhabitants die of grief."**
   —Nicholas Chamfort (1741-1794), French writer ☐ **Agree** ☐ **Disagree**

6. **"Los Angeles is a city no worse than others; a city rich and vigorous and full of pride, a city lost and beaten and full of emptiness."**
—Raymond Chandler (1888-1959), American author ☐**Agree** ☐**Disagree**

7. **"A city is a place where there is no need to wait for next week to get the answer to a question, to taste the food of any country, to find new voices to listen to and familiar ones to listen to again."**
—Margaret Mead (1901-1978), American anthropologist ☐**Agree** ☐**Disagree**

8. **"I'd rather wake up in the middle of nowhere than in any city on earth."**
—Steve McQueen (1930-1980), American actor ☐**Agree** ☐**Disagree**

9. **"The city is a human zoo, not a concrete jungle."**
—Dr. Desmond Morris (1928-), British zoologist ☐**Agree** ☐**Disagree**

10. **"The city must never be confused with the words that describe it. And yet, between one and the other, there is a connection."**
—Italo Calvino (1923-1985), Italian novelist ☐**Agree** ☐**Disagree**

Discussion: Which was your favorite quote? Why?

Pronunciation Corner

12

/th/ vs. /s/

Much like the previous chapter, Vietnamese learners of English often do not pronounce /th/ because /th/ sound does not exist in Vietnamese. Instead, they will replace /th/ with /t/ or also common, /s/. We practiced /th/ and /t/ in the previous chapter. Now we'll be practicing /th/ and /s/.

Pair work: Thumbs up, thumbs down.

Student A: Choose any word on the /th/ or /s/ words list below and say it out loud.
Student B: If Student A says a **/th/** word, Student B gives the **thumbs up** sign. If they say a /**s**/word, Student B should give the **thumbs down** sign.

When you get three thumbs up in a row, switch roles.

/th/	/s/
pa**th**	pa**ss**
fai**th**	fa**ce**
mou**th**	mou**se**
thought	**s**ought
thing	**s**ing
for**th**	for**ce**
grow**th**	gro**ss**
thank	**s**ank
thumb	**s**ome
four**th**	for**ce**
mo**th**	mo**ss**
wor**th**	wor**se**
pa**th**	pa**ss**
thin	**s**in
think	**s**ink

Culture Corner

Measurements, Dates, & Currency

Dates
Dates in the U.S. are formatted as month/day/year instead of day/month/year.
For example, January 7, 2016 can be written as:

- 1/7/2016
- 1/7/16
- 01/07/16
- 01/07/2016

Measurements
The U.S. uses the following measurements in everyday life:

- Ounces and pounds instead of grams and kilos
- Miles instead of kilometers
- Feet/yards instead of meters
- Fahrenheit instead of Celsius

Currency

The dollar is the official currency in the U.S. Be careful when shopping because the paper currency is the same size and color.

Additionally, the U.S. has coins whose value is not based on size or color.

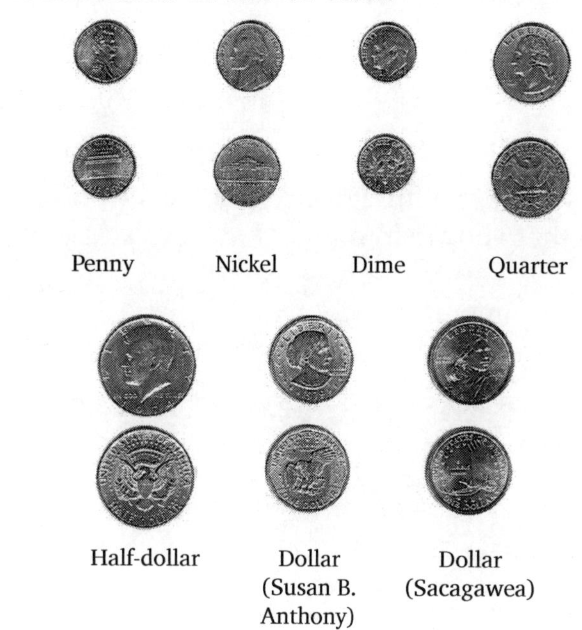

Activity 1:

Money Matters

With a partner, discuss the following questions.

1. How much is a penny? Who is on it?
2. How much is a nickel? Who is on it?
3. How much is a dime? Who is on that coin?
4. How much is a quarter? Who is on it?
5. How many cents are in a half dollar? Who is on the half-dollar coin?
6. Who is on the silver dollar coin?
7. How many dimes are in a dollar? Who is on the bronze colored dollar coin?

Activity 2:

Who are these American heroes, anyway?

Working in small groups, every student should pick a bill or a coin. Find out who is on the currency. Use your smart phone, and take a few minutes to research the American hero or icon on the bill or coin. Tell your classmates a little bit more about the traditional American hero in small groups.

Search & Share

Tripadvisor: Exploring a New City

Student Name:________________________ Date:________________________

Let's explore a foreign city together! Go to www.tripadvisor.com and type "Things to Do" in the city that you wish to visit.

Spend some time to look at the pictures and read the descriptions of the many places that you can visit while in that city. Share this information with your classmates.

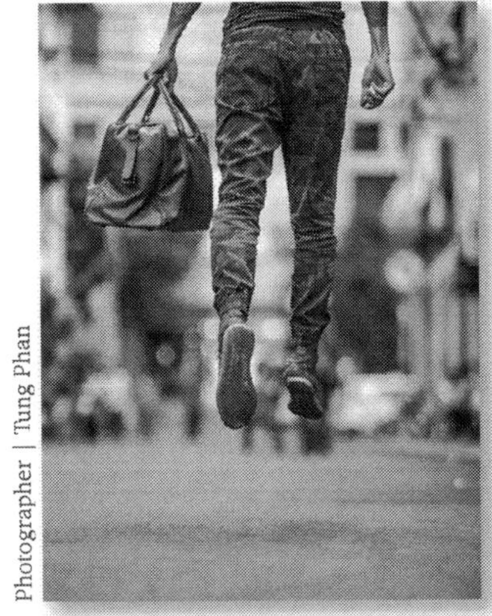

Photographer | Tung Phan

1. What city did you visit?
2. What are two facts about this city?
3. Were there any illustrations? What kind?
4. What did you learn about this city?
5. What did you learn about the country where this city is located?
6. What was the most interesting part for you? Why?
7. Write down five new vocabulary words, idioms, or expressions.
8. How would you rate the article on a scale of 1–5, with 5 being the highest? Why?
9. Why did you choose this city?
10. Are you hoping to go to this city? Why?

> **"The bold adventurer succeeds the best."**
> —Ovid (43 B.C.E.–17 C.E.) Roman poet

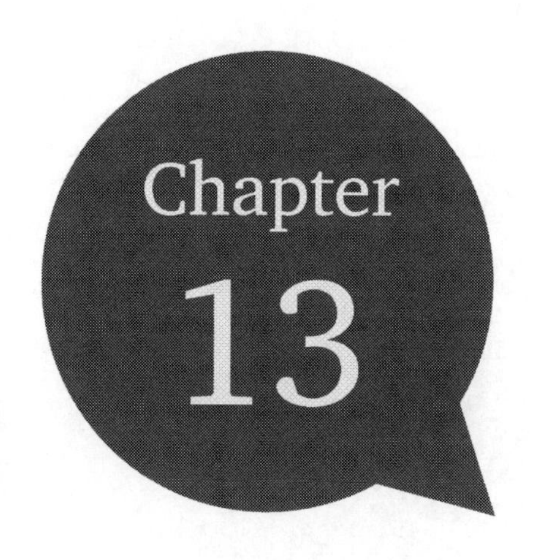

Dramatic Moments

"Talking about dreams is like talking about movies, since the cinema uses the language of dreams; years pass in a second and you can hop from one place to another."
—Federico Fellini (1920-1993), Italian film director

Photographer | Tung Phan

Getting Started

Photographer | Tung Phan

Picture Story

Directions:
Write a short story about the picture above. Who is it? What is his name? What is he doing, feeling, thinking, etc.? Share your story with your classmate(s).

Sharing Experiences

Photographer | Mindy Bao Ngoc

Movies are a great topic of conversation when meeting new people. Everybody watches movies. Even people who say they do not like movies have seen some movies, and talking about movies can be an easy way to get to know someone better. Talk with your partner and share your movie experiences.

1. Have you seen any good movies lately?
2. Where do you usually watch movies? At home, on your computer, on a tablet, or in a theater? How often do you see movies?
3. How have you changed the way you watch movies? Do you rent at a store, or do you use the Internet, cable, or satellite?
4. Which movies have you seen more than once? Which movies have you seen more than twice? Why do you like these movies so much?
5. Do you own any movies? Which ones? Do you watch them repeatedly?
6. Have you figured out a way to see movies for free? What is your secret?
7. What do you like about the movie theater experience?
8. Do you have a favorite movie theater? Where do you prefer to sit?
9. Have you ever seen a celebrity or famous actor in person? Where did this happen? What was the celebrity doing?
10. Have you ever watched a movie in English without looking at the Vietnamese subtitles? How much did you understand?
11. Which Vietnamese movie do you like the most? Why?
12. Who is your favorite actor or actress? Why?
13. Have you ever acted in a play or a movie? Can you describe your experience?
14. What do you think would be difficult about being an actor or actress?
15. Have you ever watched a movie on your smartphone or tablet? If so, how does the experience compare to seeing movies in the theater?

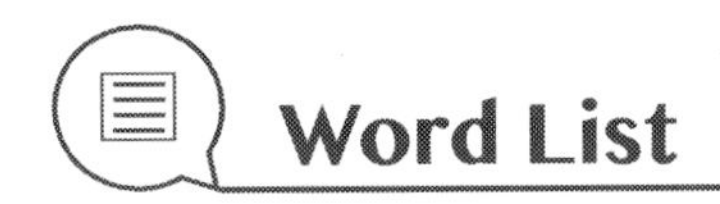

Word List

Which words do you already know? Underline them, and circle the words you are unsure about. Then review your answers with a partner.

Noun	Verb	Adjective
animation /a.ni.mê.shần/	*adapt /ờ.đáp/	famous /phê.mìs/
blockbuster **/bloc.bấs.stờ/**	**cast** **/ khás /**	popular /pop.pưu.lờ/
cast **/ khás /**	miscast /mís.khas/	blockbuster /bloc.bấs.stờ/
celebrity /xờ.le.brơ.đì/		
director /đờ.réc.tờ/		
genre /jon.rà/		
*media /me.đi.à/		
*publication /pâb.bli.khê.shần/		

*Indicates words on the Academic Word List. See p.204 for all AWL words used in this book.

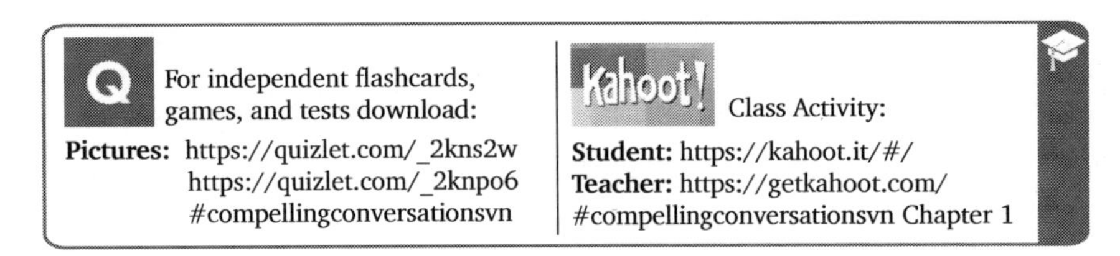

Expanding Vocabulary

adapt [verb]: to change; modify.

> **Ex:** The English novel *Oliver Twist* has been **adapted** many times into many different films; some **adaptations** have been quite successful in depicting how poverty harms children.

animation [noun]: a moving cartoon, a technique used to make drawings seem alive.

> Ex: Both children and adults love the **animation** films Finding Dory and The Lion King.

blockbuster [noun]: a very popular movie, often with expensive special effects.
[adjective]: pertaining to a major success.

> Ex: **Blockbusters** often require a large financial investment.
> The **blockbuster** Avatar made over $1 billion, used fantastic special effects, and inspired millions of movie fans.

cast [noun]: the actors in a play, show or movie.
[verb]: to assign a role in a show.

> Ex: The Harry Potter series has a great **cast** of British actors and actresses.

celebrity [noun]: a famous person; a person who attracts media attention.

> Ex: After the movie Titanic, actress Kate Winslet became a **celebrity**.

director [noun]: the person who directs the actors and crew in the making of a film. They control a film's artistic and dramatic aspects.

> Ex: Stephen Spielberg is among the world's most famous **directors**.

famous [adjective]: well-known, recognized by most people.

> Ex: Hạ Long Bay, a UNESCO World Heritage site, is **famous** for its stunning beauty.

genre [noun]: category of artistic endeavor having a particular form, content, or technique.

> Ex: Romantic comedies are my favorite **genre**, but my boyfriend prefers action films.

media [noun]: an organized system where an idea is communicated or information is circulated.

> Ex: The **media** coverage of entertainment awards shows usually lasts for a week.

miscast [verb]: placing the wrong actor in a role.

> Ex: Do you think George Clooney was **miscast** as Batman?

popular [adjective]: well-liked, regarded with affection.

> Ex: Fast and Furious has been a very **popular** film series worldwide.

publication [noun] a widely-circulated book, magazine or journal.

> **Ex:** The magazine *Smithsonian* remains an influential **publication.**

Movie Genres

- Action • Adventure • Animation • Biography
- Children • Comedy• Crime/Detective • Documentary
- Drama • Epic • Fantasy • Foreign
- Historical • Horror • Melodrama • Musical
- Mystery • Romance • Romantic Comedy• Silent
- Science Fiction • Suspense • War • Western

? Asking Questions with New Vocabulary Words

A. Select five vocabulary words in this chapter and write a question for each word. Remember to start your question with a question word (Who, What, Where, When, Why, How, Is, Are, Do, Did, Does, etc.). End each question with a question mark (?). Underline each vocabulary word.

Example: *Can you name a famous actor?*

1. ______________________________
2. ______________________________
3. ______________________________
4. ______________________________
5. ______________________________

B. Take turns asking and answering questions with your partner or group members. Ask your instructor to check your English grammar.

13

Paraphrasing Proverbs

Read the following proverbs and discuss them with your partner. Write what you think they mean in the spaces provided. Circle your favorites. Explain your choices.

Vietnamese:

Ants persistently working will fill their nests.
"Kiến tha lâu cũng đầy tổ."
Meaning: ______________________________

If you waste heaven's gifts, you won't have anything for ten lives.
"Phí của trời, mười đời chẳng có."
Meaning: ______________________________

Actions speak louder than words.
"Làm hay hơn nói."
Meaning: ______________________________

International:

Spectators see better than actors. —Persian
Meaning: ______________________________

Perseverance brings success. —Dutch
Meaning: ______________________________

Put faith in your own abilities and not in the stars. —Japanese
Meaning: ______________________________

It takes ten years to become an overnight success. —American
Meaning: ______________________________

We're fools whether we dance or not, so we may as well dance. —English
Meaning: ______________________________

The Conversation Continues

Duong Trinh | @minhduongtrinh94

Let's continue to explore topics related to exploring cities with one or two classmates. Use complete sentences to respond.

1. Which genres of movies do you enjoy? Why?
2. What makes your favorite films so special or memorable?
3. Name a few movies you disliked. Why did you dislike them? Did you walk out on them in the theater or stop watching them at home?
4. What are some books that have been adapted into movies? Did the adaptations work?
5. What was your favorite movie as a child? What movie did you like most as a teenager?
6. Who was your favorite movie star as a child? Why was this person your favorite? Do you still like this star?
7. Have you ever had a "crush" on a movie star?
8. Approximately how many movies do you watch in a year? Do you pay attention to word of mouth? How do you decide which movies you want to see?
9. Do you read movie reviews? Do you enjoy watching previews and movie trailers? Why?
10. Do you eat snacks when you watch movies? What do you eat?
11. Which actors, actresses, or directors would you like to have lunch with? What would you ask them?

12. Do you have any favorite directors? What is their filmmaking style?
13. In your opinion, what makes a good movie? Can you give an example?
14. Can you give an example of a great movie? What is the difference for you between a good and a great movie?
15. Which movies would you suggest to visitors to see? Why?

Building Words

Using the Latin Prefix "pre-"

Even the word prefix begins with a prefix! If you look closely at "prefix," you will see this the prefix "pre" which means "before." We can find this popular prefix in many places from the previews for future movies to preschools for young children.

Prefix	Meaning	Example
pre-	before	"Pre**judge**" means to judge before you have information.

Complete the chart.

Prefix	Base	New Word
pre-	fix	*prefix*
pre-	approved	
pre-	caution	
pre-	cooked	
pre-	dawn	
pre-	dominant	
pre-	law	
pre-	mature	
pre-	pay	
pre-	packaged	
pre-	test	
pre-		
pre-		

13

A. Select four words from the above chart and create a question for your partner. Remember to start your question with a question word (Who, What, Where, When, Why, How, Is, Are, Do, Did, Does, etc.). End each question with a question mark (?). Underline each vocabulary word.

1. ______________________________
2. ______________________________
3. ______________________________
4. ______________________________

B. Take turns asking and answering questions with your partner. Ask your English teacher to give you feedback to check your English grammar.

Discussing Quotations

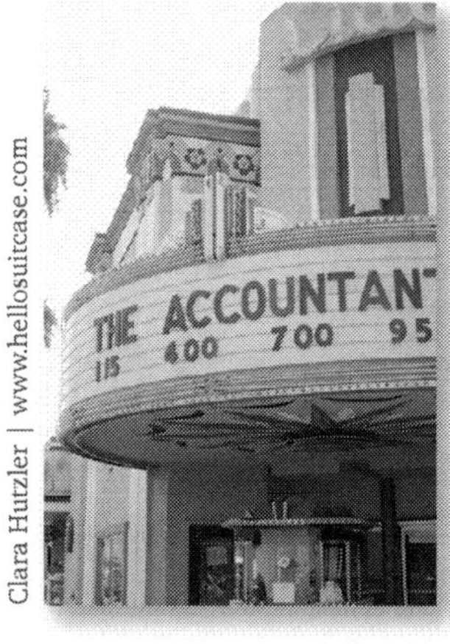

Clara Hutzler | www.hellosuitcase.com

In your small groups, take turns reading these quotations out loud and discuss them. Do you agree with the quotation? Disagree? Why? Mark your opinion. Afterwards, pick a favorite quotation. Remember to give a reason or an example.

1. **"Movies are a fad. Audiences really want to see live actors on a stage."**
—Charlie Chaplin (1889–1977), British actor ☐Agree ☐Disagree

2. **"You know what your problem is? It's that you haven't seen enough movies—all of life's riddles are answered in the movies."**
—Steve Martin (1945–), American actor/comedian ☐Agree ☐Disagree

3. **"Watch this if you like, and if you don't, take a hike."**
—Clint Eastwood (1930–), American actor/director/producer ☐Agree ☐Disagree

5. **"We need families to start taking more responsibility in understanding which movie is good for their children and which movie is not."**
—Jet Li (1963–), Chinese actor/martial artist ☐Agree ☐Disagree

13

6. **"Movies are fun, but they're not a cure for cancer."**
—Warren Beatty (1937–), American actor/director/producer
☐ **Agree** ☐ **Disagree**

7. **"I did a women's movie, and I'm not a woman. I did a gay movie, and I'm not gay. I learned as I went along."**
—Ang Lee (1954–), American director
☐ **Agree** ☐ **Disagree**

8. **"Maybe every other American movie shouldn't be based on a comic book."**
—Bill Maher (1956–), American comedian
☐ **Agree** ☐ **Disagree**

9. **"Life is like a movie, write your own ending. Keep believing, keep pretending."**
—Jim Henson (1936–1990), American creator of the Muppets
☐ **Agree** ☐ **Disagree**

10. **"The difference between life and the movies is that a script has to make sense, and life doesn't."**
—Joseph L. Mankiewicz (1909–1993), American screenwriter
☐ **Agree** ☐ **Disagree**

Discussion: Which was your favorite quote? Why?

____

____

____

Pronunciation Corner

/r/ vs. /l/

When pronouncing /r/, air flows out along the middle of the tongue without stopping. Do not let the tip of the tongue touch the roof of your mouth. When pronouncing /l/, the tip of the tongue touches the tooth ridge at the front of the mouth, and air flows out each side.

Pair work: Right hand, left hand.
Add three words that you often use that have a /r/ and /l/ sound.

Student A: Choose any word on the /r/ or /l/ words list below and say it out loud.
Student B: If Student A says a **/r/** word, Student B raises his/her **right** hand. If they say a **/l/** word, Student B raises his/her **left** hand.

When you get three thumbs up in a row, switch roles.

/l/	/r/
alive	arrive
fly	fry
long	wrong
collect	correct
law	raw
lead	read
light	rite
led	red
lot	rot
belly	berry
blue	brew
clown	crown
lack	rack
clash	crash
splint	sprint
roll	roar
fail	fair
loyal	royal
lamb	ram

Culture Corner

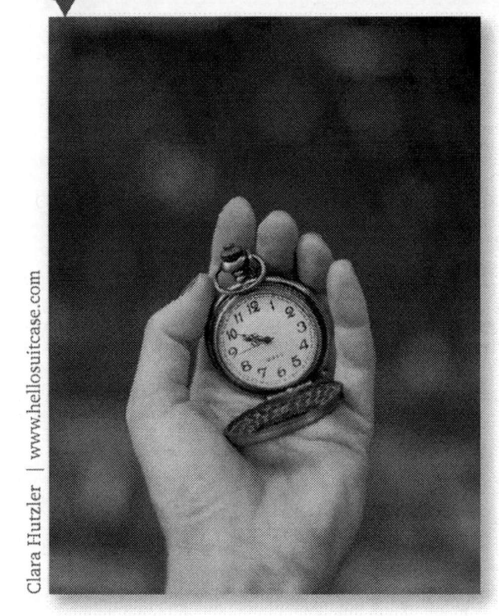
Clara Hutzler | www.hellosuitcase.com

Perception of Time

Americans live and breathe the phrase, "Time is money." Time is often perceived as a critical commodity, an item that can actually be bought or sold. We also normally associate phrases used with money in a bank to time. For instance, many Americans will talk about "saving time," "spending time," and "wasting time." In other words, most Americans highly value their time. We hate to wait!

Being on time matters. Many Americans use punctuality to judge a person's character too. For instance, if you arrive on-time to an appointment, you may be seen as a trustworthy, dependable person. If you arrive late to an appointment without calling or texting ahead, it can hurt your reputation and relationships. It could indicate that you don't respect the other person's time. Many Americans keep a busy schedule and some will feel insulted if you make them wait. Being on time is especially important in business and college, where punctuality is expected as a professional or as a student.

If you go to a public event (e.g. a movie, show, sporting event), you should arrive at least a few minutes before the scheduled time. The show will go on whether you are there or not! Luckily, this strictness does not apply to large social meetings such as a party at someone's home. You are not expected to arrive exactly on time, but you should still try to stay within a 15 to 30 minute range of the expected arrival time.

Suggestions

1. Strive to arrive on time, or even 10-15 minutes early.
2. If you know that you will be arriving late, call or text ahead of time to let others know of the delay and offer an explanation.
3. As soon as you know that you won't be able to make your appointment, immediately cancel or rearrange with the other person.

Activity: With a partner, discuss the following questions related to time.

A. What do you do if you show up early for something?
B. What do you do if you show up late for something?
C. What do you do if you forget an appointment?
D. When is it acceptable to be late?
E. When is it not acceptable to be late?
F. Does waiting for someone bother you?
G. If you had the power to stop and restart time, when would you use it?

Search & Share

Be a Movie Critic

Duong Trinh | @minhduongtrinh94

Student Name: ______________________

Date: ______________________

Can you recommend an excellent movie? First, select one of your favorite films. Second, go to **www.imdb.com** and research your selected film. Third, take notes. A strong movie review will combine both facts and opinions. Use this short worksheet to describe the movie and prepare to share your informed opinion with your classmates.

Video Title: ______________________ Length: ______________________

Genre/Date: ______________________ Director: ______________________

Actors/Actresses: ______________________ Awards: ______________________

How many times have you watched the movie? Where?

1. Where does the movie take place?
2. When does the movie take place?
3. Who are the main characters? Can you briefly describe them?
4. What happens in the movie?
5. What makes the movie interesting?
6. What is the best part? Why?
7. Does the movie surprise the audience? How? How could it be a better film?
8. How did you feel when the movie ended? Why?
9. Who do you think would like this movie? Why?
10. On a scale of 1–5 stars, with 5 being the highest, how do you rate this movie? Why?

> **"Every great film should seem new every time you see it."**
> —Roger Ebert (1942–2013), American film critic

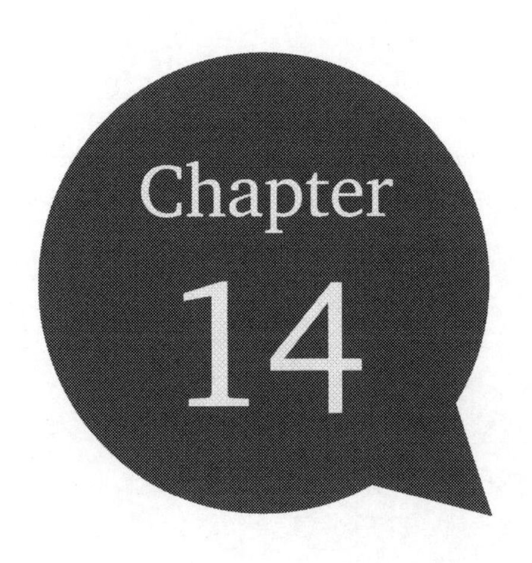

Chapter 14 Expressing Opinions

"Conversations means being able to disagree and still continue the conversation."
—Dwight MacDonald (1906-1982), American editor

Donovan Bui | www.donovanbui.com

Getting Started

Photographer | Tung Phan

Corner Conversations

Directions:
Let's have conversations about possible issues that you could have with different groups of people. Choose the topic you would like to talk about first and stand in that corner of the room. Students in the same corner of the room should have a conversation about their topic. When prompted, change corners to have a different conversation with other students about a new topic.

What are some issues that you could have with your…

Corner 1: Friends	Corner 3: Family
______________ ______________ ______________	______________ ______________ ______________
Corner 2: Classmates	**Corner 4: Co-workers**
______________ ______________ ______________	______________ ______________ ______________

Sharing Experiences

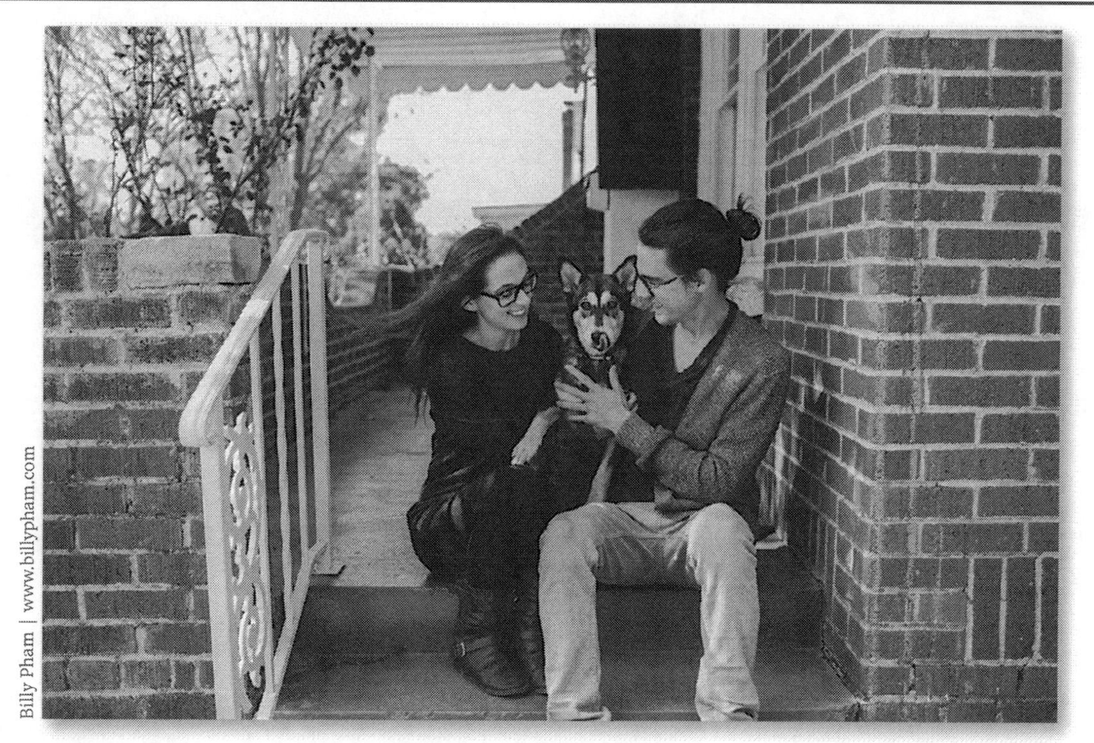

Billy Pham | www.billypham.com

Harmony is often important, but sometimes we still find ourselves disagreeing with loved ones, close friends, and co-workers. Therefore, we have to find ways to resolve the conflict in a respectful way. Sometimes we just listen and postpone an awkward discussion. Sometimes we try to find agreement and focus on where we agree. And sometimes we need to identify and express our disagreement so we can solve problems together.

1. Are you a good listener? Why do you say that?
2. When are you most likely to share your opinions? Why?
3. What topics do you like to discuss with your friends?
4. What do you usually talk about with your family?
5. When was the last time you had a disagreement over an opinion?
6. How did you resolve this disagreement?
7. How do you feel about conflict?
8. How often do you speak up for yourself?
9. What do you think is a common cause of conflict between friends?
10. When was the last time you compromised with someone?
11. Do you feel more comfortable compromising or fighting? Why?
12. Do you consider yourself stubborn? Why or why not?
13. Do you find it hard to apologize? Why or Why not?
14. When was the last time you were proven right in an argument or debate?
15. Do other people come to you with their problems? Why do you think that is?

Here are some common expressions that allow you to agree or disagree in **casual** conversations. Read all phrases aloud.

Expressing Agreement	Expressing Disagreement
Yep.	Nope.
You got it!	You lost me.
I hear you!	I don't think so!
You're so right!	You're so wrong!
That's right!	That's just wrong!

But sometimes it is more useful to use more careful phrases to you can keep the conversation friendly while politely disagreeing with a friend, co-worker, or even relative. Read all phrases aloud.

Expressing Agreement	Politely Disagreement
Sure	Perhaps.
Absolutely...	I partially agree.
That's true...	That doesn't seem completely true.
I believe that...	Sorry, I don't share that belief.
That's a good idea...	Is that really a good idea?
This explains A, B, and C...	Have you thought about X, Y, or Z?
That's right on point...	That seems a bit off point.
I concur...	Sorry, I can't completely agree.
I agree...	I guess I sort of disagree.
That's makes sense...	Does that really make sense?
I accept that...	I reject that.
I support...	I can't support that right now.
That's a good idea!	Here's a better idea!
I definitely agree...	I'm not sure I agree.
You should agree with me...	We agree on some points.
That sounds logical...	Is that really logical?
It's simple...	Or is it complicated?

Culture Corner

Small Talk

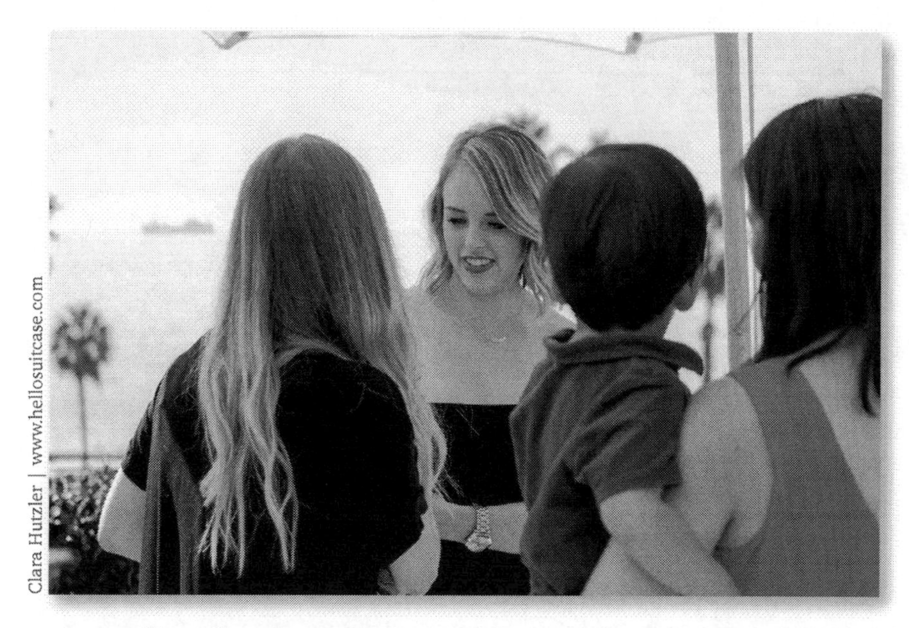

Clara Hutzler | www.hellosuitcase.com

Americans love to have friendly conversations without a clear purpose beyond positive feelings and general curiosity. This communication is known as "small talk," and helps build relationships. As a result, Americans often don't wait to be introduced and will begin to speak with strangers. Sometimes they will even share personal stories as they stand in line or sit next to strangers at an event. Don't be surprised at this informality. Be confident and try to be straight to the point as quickly as possible. Don't be afraid to be more direct and more honest than you might act in your native language or home country. Small talk usually follows the English conversation advice: "be light, bright, and polite." American small talk also tends to be causal and cheerful.

Small Talk Topics

1. Start conversation by flashing a big smile to the stranger and asking, "How are you?" However, keep in mind that this is simply a greeting and is not a question about your health. If you are asked this question, don't give a detailed account of your health history. Just give a short, positive response: "I'm good."

2. Never ask a new American acquaintance a direct question about their salary, religion, age, money, or weight. In addition, do not make any racist or negative remarks about someone's religion, family background, or lifestyle. Be light, bright, and polite.

Activity 1: With a partner, add 5 possible topics for small talk.

1. ______________________________
2. ______________________________
3. ______________________________
4. ______________________________
5. ______________________________

Activity 2: Write a friendly question for each of these topics.

1. ______________________________
2. ______________________________
3. ______________________________
4. ______________________________
5. ______________________________

Activity 3: Turn to a partner and practice small talk.

Word List

Which words do you already know? Underline them, and circle the words you are unsure about. Then review your answers with a partner.

Noun	Verb	Adjective
acceptance /ạc.xép.tins/	accept /ạc.xép/	ambivalent /èm.bia.vơ.lện/
consequence /khon.sơ.khuânx/	***advocate /át.vơ.khệt/**	
solution /sờ.lu.shần/	*assume /ờ.xum/	
*controversy /khon.chô.vơ.sì/	concur /khần.khơ/	
***advocate /át.vơ.khệt/**	prejudge /pre.jờ.đis/	
	solve /xov/	
	*resolve /rì.zov/	

*Indicates words on the Academic Word List. See p.204 for all AWL words used in this book.

14

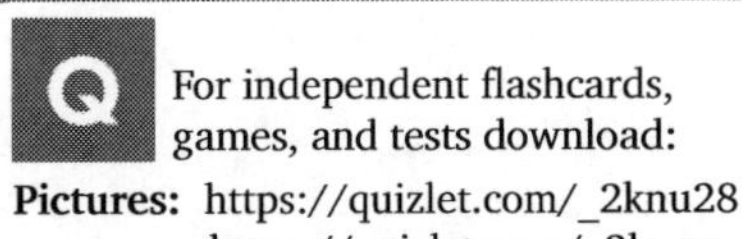

For independent flashcards, games, and tests download:

Pictures: https://quizlet.com/_2knu28
https://quizlet.com/_2knscq
#compellingconversationsvn

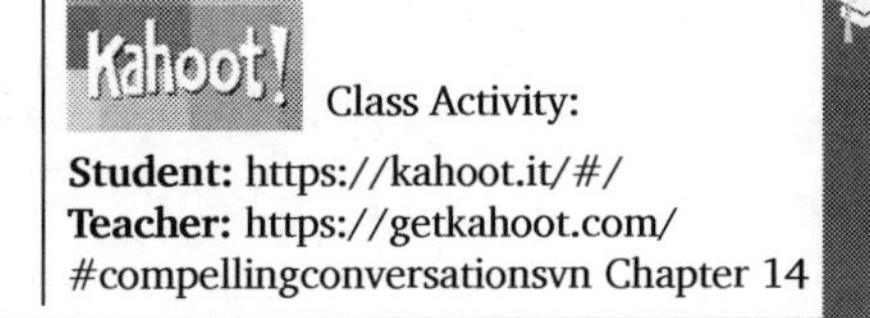

Class Activity:

Student: https://kahoot.it/#/
Teacher: https://getkahoot.com/
#compellingconversationsvn Chapter 14

Expanding Vocabulary

Look at the definitions and example sentences below. Do the definitions match what you and your partner expected in the Word List? If not, what is different?

accept [verb]: to say yes, to agree, to concur.

> Ex: Ngọc Sương **accepted** the invitation to dinner.

acceptance [noun]: the act of agreeing, the act of receiving something offered.

> Ex: Her **acceptance** of his marriage proposal made everyone smile.

advocate [verb]: to argue for something or someone, to urge people to act.
[noun]: a person who argues for something or someone.

> Ex: She **advocates** using smartphones in more English classrooms.
> The young lawyer became an effective **advocate** for her client.

ambivalent [adjective]: to have mixed, conflicting feelings.

> Ex: I'm **ambivalent** because it's a complicated situation; I have mixed feelings.

assume [verb]: to accept without evidence, to believe without question.

> Ex: Let's **assume** that all parents love their children and they always want the best for them.

concur [verb]: to agree with, to support.

> Ex: Quỳnh Trang **concurred** with his co-workers that they were lucky to have good jobs.

consequence [noun]: the result or outcome of something.

> Ex: Tú's decision to move to Phú Quốc had many **consequences**.

controversy [noun]: a heavily debated issue, a public discussion with opposing sides.

> **Ex:** She got caught up in a **controversy** after she made inappropriate accusations on live television.

prejudge [verb]: to assume, to judge before knowing.

> **Ex:** It's often a mistake to **prejudge** social events; sometimes we enjoy activities that we expected to dislike.

resolve [verb]: to reach a solution or make a formal decision.

> **Ex:** Tùng and Vy haven't **resolved** their disagreement yet; they need more time.

solve [verb]: to find the answer, to work something out.

> **Ex:** Engineers **solve** problems by examining facts, considering alternatives, and making calculations.

solution [noun]: the act of solving problems, finding answers.

> **Ex:** The simplest **solution** is sometimes the best solution, but sometimes the simplest solution doesn't really solve the problem.

? Asking Questions with New Vocabulary Words

A. Select five vocabulary words in this chapter and write a question for each word. Remember to start your question with a question word (Who, What, Where, When, Why, How, Is, Are, Do, Did, Does, etc.). You also want to end each question with a question mark (?). Underline each vocabulary word.

Example: *Is that assumption reasonable?*

1. ______
2. ______
3. ______
4. ______
5. ______

B. Take turns asking and answering questions with your partner or group members. Ask your instructor to give you feedback on your questions to check your English grammar.

Discussing Proverbs

Do you agree or disagree with the following proverbs? Or do you have mixed feelings and feel ambivalent? Why? Discuss with your partner.

1. The best things in life are free.	☐ **Agree**	☐ **Disagree**	☐ **Ambivalent**
2. Money is the root of all evil.	☐ **Agree**	☐ **Disagree**	☐ **Ambivalent**
3. Children should be seen and not heard.	☐ **Agree**	☐ **Disagree**	☐ **Ambivalent**
4. Spare the rod and spoil the child.	☐ **Agree**	☐ **Disagree**	☐ **Ambivalent**
5. Honesty is the best policy.	☐ **Agree**	☐ **Disagree**	☐ **Ambivalent**
6. It's better to have loved and lost than never to have loved at all.	☐ **Agree**	☐ **Disagree**	☐ **Ambivalent**
7. Behind every successful man, there's a woman.	☐ **Agree**	☐ **Disagree**	☐ **Ambivalent**
8. The ends justifies the means.	☐ **Agree**	☐ **Disagree**	☐ **Ambivalent**
9. Winning is everything.	☐ **Agree**	☐ **Disagree**	☐ **Ambivalent**
10. Persistence pays.	☐ **Agree**	☐ **Disagree**	☐ **Ambivalent**

Choose a proverb from the previous section about which you and your conversation partner disagree. Spend five minutes thinking of situations to support your point of view. Then discuss your opinions in a friendly, respectful way. Use some of the phrases at the beginning of this chapter to keep the conversation flowing. Write down the proverb that you will discuss.

Discussing Proverbs Continued

A. Consider each of the following common statements, attitudes, or proverbs. Which statement of agreement or disagreement best expresses your reaction?

- Seeing is believing.
- Appearances are deceiving.
- Beauty promises happiness.
- Be good and you will be happy.
- No pain, no gain. .
- The bigger, the better.

- Less is more.
- Expect the unexpected.
- The sun rises every morning.
- You get what you pay for.
- A penny saved is a penny earned.
- Bad news travels fast.
- Liars should have good memories.
- Counting your money is how you keep score.
- Time heals all wounds.
- Never forget; never forgive.
- Don't throw your pearls before swine.
- A donkey prefers hay to gold.
- The early bird catches the worm.
- Two heads are better than one.

B. We've studied proverbs throughout this book. Ask five questions using a proverb.

Example: *Do you agree that time heals all wounds?*

1. ______________________________
2. ______________________________
3. ______________________________
4. ______________________________
5. ______________________________

Remember

- Make notes
- Ask questions
- Find solutions

Building Words

Putting It together: "Form"

Let's take a single word, and see how we can build a stronger academic vocabulary from a single word: "form." Form means shape, which can be a verb or a noun.

Many prefixes can go before "form." Underline the prefix.

1. Perform
2. Inform
3. Reform
4. Deform
5. Conform
6. Transform

Let's add the suffix "-ed' to make the past tense of these seven verbs. Can you think of five other words that come from the word "form?" You might want to use some of the prefixes and suffixes that you have studied in this book and over the years.

Consult a dictionary and your teacher to check your answers. Hint: There are many, many possible answers!

Word	Suffix	New Word
form	**-ed**	*formed*
perform	**-ed**	
inform	**-ed**	
reform	**-ed**	
deform	**-ed**	
conform	**-ed**	
transform	**-ed**	

A. Select four words from the above chart and create a question for your partner. Remember to start your question with a question word (Who, What, Where, When, Why, How, Is, Are, Do, Did, Does, etc.). End each question with a question mark (?). Underline each vocabulary word.

1. ________________________________
2. ________________________________
3. ________________________________
4. ________________________________

B. Take turns asking and answering questions with your partner. Ask your instructor to give you feedback on your questions to check your English grammar.

The Conversation Continues

Clara Hutzler | www.hellosuitcase.com

Sometimes we have to have difficult conversations. Sometimes we discuss problems about work, school, city, and country. Sometimes we agree and sometimes we disagree with our friends, relatives, co-workers, and classmates.

Here are some topics that people can discuss. Pick two or three topics and examine the social issues with your classmates.

1. Why does cheating occur in some schools?
2. What is another problem in public schools today?
3. What is a problem in your neighborhood? What do you think can be done? Why?
4. Do you consider traffic a major problem? Why?
5. What might be some possible solutions to traffic jams?
6. What are some environmental problems? Why?
7. What can be done to improve the situation?
8. How can parents get their children to do better in school?
9. What are difficulties for people living in big cities?
10. What are some difficulties for people living in the countryside today?
11. How can cities reduce crime? Why?
12. Do you think we should increase the number of international students on campus?
13. How can colleges help prepare people to lead happier, healthier lives?
14. What are some economic problems today?
15. How does immigration help the United States economy?
16. What do you think the government can do to improve the health habits of citizens?
17. Should there be a special tax on sodas and candy?
18. What can we do to prevent future terrorist attacks? Why?
19. What do you see as the three biggest problems in our country? Why?
20. Why do you think so many people don't get enough sleep?

Discussing Quotations

In your small groups, take turns reading these quotations out loud and discuss them. Do you agree with the quotation? Disagree? Why? Mark your opinion. Afterwards, pick a favorite quotation. Remember to give a reason or an example.

1. **"True love is like ghosts, which everybody talks about and few have seen."**
   —Francois Duc De La Rochefoucauld (1613-1680), French writer — ☐**Agree** ☐**Disagree**

2. **"Do not anticipate trouble or worry about what may never happen. Keep in the sunlight."**
   —Benjamin Franklin (1705-1790), American states man/scientist — ☐**Agree** ☐**Disagree**

3. **"Nobody minds having what is too good for them."**
   —Jane Austen (1775-1821), English novelist — ☐**Agree** ☐**Disagree**

4. **"Nothing is so dangerous as an ignorant friend; a wise enemy is much better."**
   —Jean de La Fontaine (1621-1695), French poet — ☐**Agree** ☐**Disagree**

5. **"Argument is the worst form of conversation."**
   —Jonathon Swift (1667–1745), English writer — ☐**Agree** ☐**Disagree**

6. **"It was the best of times; it was the worst of times."**
   —Charles Dickens (1812-1870), English novelist — ☐**Agree** ☐**Disagree**

7. **"If two ride on a horse, one must ride behind."**
   —William Shakespeare (1564-1616), English playwright — ☐**Agree** ☐**Disagree**

8. **"Experience is the name everyone gives their mistakes."**
   —Oscar Wilde (1854-1900), Irish playwright — ☐**Agree** ☐**Disagree**

9. **"It is only with the heart that one can see rightly; what is essential is invisible to the eye."**
   — Antoine de Saint-Exupery (1900 – 1944), French writer/pilot — ☐**Agree** ☐**Disagree**

10. **"A problem is a chance for you to do your best."**
    —Duke Ellington (1890-1974), Jazz composer — ☐**Agree** ☐**Disagree**

Discussion: Which was your favorite quote? Why?

Pronunciation Corner

Final Sound: -ed Endings in Verbs

–ed endings for regular verbs is one of the most confusing ending sounds for Vietnamese speakers because it has three different pronunciations for the same written expression. When –ed is part of the past tense of a regular verb, it can be pronounced as /d/, /t/, or /+syllable/ depending on the last sound of the root verb.

If the root verb ends in one of these sounds	Example of root verb	–ed example	-ed sound
voiced	play	played **/playd/**	/d/
voiceless	laugh	laughed **/lăft/**	/t/
/t/ or /d/	want	wanted **/woanh.tid/**	/+syllable/

Pair work: Put the following words in the correct column. Practice saying the words

acted	cried	folded	needed	hoped	hunted
asked	crowded	followed	placed	spelled	watched
baked	ended	laughed	planned	hiked	wished
called	filled	aged	played	stopped	wrapped
loved	floated	melted	seemed	rented	

/d/	/t/	/+syllable/

14

Classroom Activity: Role-Play

Seeking Clarification

Photographer | Mindy Bao Ngoc

Sometimes we need more information to better understand each other and reach an agreement. Asking the right questions can help us achieve that. The following phrases are some sample questions that you can ask to seek clarification. Read each of these phrases aloud to your partner.

- Can you clarify that?
  /Khèn du kle.ri.phài đát?/
- Can you explain your ideas more?
  /Khèn du èx.plên dò ai.đia mor?/
- What do you mean?
  /Wắt đù du min?/
- What do you mean by that?
  /Wắt đù du min bài đát?/
- Can you rephrase that?
  /Khèn du rì.phrê.z đát?/
- Why do you say that?
  /Woai đù du xê đát?/
- Can you give another example?
  /Khèn du giv ờ.no.đờ ès.zem.bồ?/
- Have you considered?
  /Hav du khẩn.xia.đờ?/
- What if the situation were a bit different?
  /Wắt if đờ xít.chu.ê.shần wờ ờ biết đíf.phận?/
- What if?
  /Wắt if?/
- How far would you go?
  /Hao phar wuật du ghô?/
- Are you sure? Why are you so sure?
  /Àr du suâ? Wai àr du xô suâ?/
- What's your source for that bit of information?
  /Wắt.s dòr xór.s phòr đát biết ôv in.phớ.mây.shần?/
- How do you know?
  /Hao đù du nô?/
- Can you imagine some alternatives?
  /Khèn du ìm.ma.jìn xâm ào.thơ.na.thìv.z?/
- Is there another possibility?
  /Ìz đè ờ.na.đờ pós.sờ.bil.la.đi?/

14

"Anyone who stops learning is old, whether at twenty or eighty. Anyone who keeps learning stays young."
—Henry Ford (1863-1947), American industrialist

Classroom Activity

Problem-Solution Worksheet

The English proverb "Two heads are better than one" is often true. Solving problems can frequently be difficult. Working with your partners, focus on a problem—at school, at work, or in the local city—and find a reasonable solution together. Follow this widely used problem solution method. You can also use the 5W (who, what, where, when, why, and how) filter in this exercise. Sharing detailed, precise information is an important skill in academic and professional situations. Be ready to share your process and conclusions with your other classmates. You might even be asked to give a short presentation too!

Define the Problem:

1. What's the background?

2. What's the problem?

3. What are some short-term effects resulting from this problem?

4. What are some long-term effects resulting from this problem?

Find the Best Solution:

1. What is a possible solution?
    a. What would be an advantage of this solution?

    b. What would be a disadvantage?

2. What is another possible solution?
    a. What would be an advantage of this solution?

    b. What would be a disadvantage?

3. Is there a third possible solution?
    a. What would be an advantage of this solution?

    b. What would be a disadvantage?

14

Of these solutions, which do you think is the best? Provide three reasons.

1. ______________________________
2. ______________________________
3. ______________________________

> **"In the middle of a difficulty lies an opportunity."**
> —Albert Einstein (1879-1955),
> Time Magazine 'Man of the 20th Century'

Search & Share

TED Talk

Student Name:________________________ Date:________________________

Have you heard about TED (Technology, Entertainment, and Design) talks yet? These "riveting talks by remarkable people, free to the world", according to the TED.com website, come from global experts in many disciplines. The presenters give highly personal presentations that address many important and some entertaining topics in short, engaging talks. Themes range from business, education, and technology to culture, science, and development. Find a short video on a topic of particular interest to you. Although lectures can be seen as a one-way conversation, the best TED talks show us how to share specialized information in a comfortable, effective, and friendly manner. You will probably want to watch and listen to the talk two times before answering these questions. Finally, be prepared to review the TED talk for your classmates in a series of small group discussions. Please answer the following questions to start preparing your review:

1 What is the title of the talk?

2 Who is the speaker? What is the speaker's background?

3 Where and when was the TED talk given?

4 How did the speaker begin the presentation?

5 What is the theme of the talk? Does it match the title? How?

6 What was a memorable part of this TED talk? What made it memorable?

7 How did the speaker connect to his audience? (Humor, visual aids, etc)

8 What did the speaker want to accomplish? Do you think the speaker achieved their goals?

9 Did the speaker convince you? Why?

10 Why did you choose this TED talk?

10 How would you rate this TED talk on a scale of 1-5? Why?

14

"We only think when confronted with a problem."
— John Dewey (1859- 1952), American philosopher and educational reformer

Answer Key

P. 47 Chapter 4: Being Home

Student B: Listen carefully to your partner's description. Draw the description you hear in the box

Partner B:

P. 90 Chapter 7: Habits and Routines

1. Alabama Section 32-5A-53
2. Alaska 13.25.050 Possession of air guns and similar devices.
3. California The ordinance (Refer to Chapter 9.10, Part 13)
4. F
5. Georgia O.C.G.A. Section 12-5-288
6. Hawaii §445-112
7. Louisiana Acts 1974, No. 553, § 1.
8. F
9. Texas § 48.02.
10. Washington RCW 70.98.170

Source: http://www.dumblaws.com/

APPENDIX

We want you to speak as much English as possible, both in and outside of your English classes. These extra materials can be used to deepen the classroom experience, for homework, or for self-study. These bonus materials are optional and supplemental—but clearly recommended.

Time restrictions and class sizes often limit the use of these supplemental activities. Many chapters include opportunities for students to give brief presentations. Feedback is helpful so we can learn what our audience heard and thought. Therefore, we have included forms for both instructor and peer feedback. Peer feedback forms provide valuable information. Peer evaluation remains a common classroom assignment in many American universities. It's also a best practice in numberous academic high schools and English language programs. It's also considered a recommended "best practice" internationally because the entire audience can ask questions, share ideas, and provide student to student feedback.

We hope that you choose to speak English more outside of the English classroom "in the real world." Sometimes planning a conversation in advance makes it easier. The surveys here provide a "map" for short, comfortable English conversations with international tourists. The surveys are arranged from simplest to the most difficult. Use these bonus worksheets to continually improve your English and create your own compelling conversations both inside and outside the classroom.

"All's well that ends well."
—William Shakespeare (1564–1616), play wright and poet

Search & Share

Reviewing Stress Patterns in English

Student Name: ______________________ Date: ______________________

Find a video that gives tips or suggestions on common word stress patterns in English. Stress patterns are very important in improving the pronunciation of English words and sentences. Better understanding stress patterns in English will help you be better understood in English. Watch the video, carefully listen, take notes, and share the pronunciation tips with your classmates.

Video Title: ______________________ Length: ______________________

Web Address: ______________________ Creator: ______________________

1. Describe the video.
2. What pronunciation tips did the video give?
3. Which words or sounds did the video focus on?
4. How practical did you find the advice? Why?
5. What was the strongest part? Why?
6. What was the weakest part? Why?
7. Who do you think is the target audience for this video? Why?
8. Why did you choose this video?
9. Do you think this video will help improve your pronunciation of English words?
10. How would you rate this video on a scale of 1–5, with 5 being the highest? Why?

"We learn by doing."
– English proverb

Search & Share

Independent Reading Log

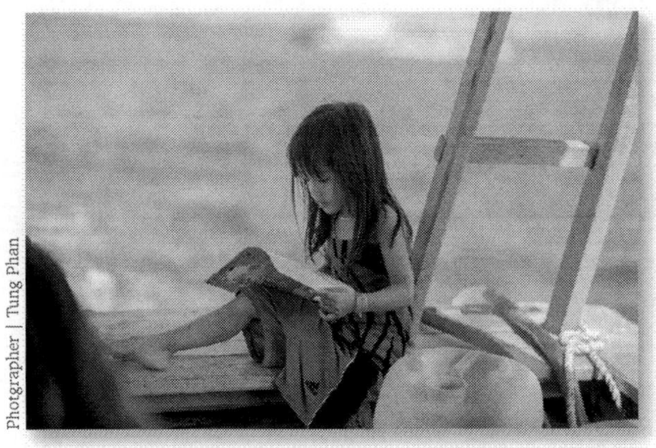
Photographer | Tung Phan

Demonstrate your knowledge of reading by exploring how you read, what you read, and what you think when you read. Then practice your conversation skills by sharing what you read.

Share the following with a partner:

- Title and author of the article you read for the from **https://www.dogonews.com/**
- At **least** ONE answer from the HOW YOU READ selection
- At **least** TWO answers from the WHAT YOU READ selection
- At **least** ONE answer from the WHAT YOU THINK selection

Answer in complete sentences with specific details to support your answer. You may choose any prompt to answer—there may be some questions you never answer, and some you answer each week. If you choose to repeat a question, be sure you answer it in a different way that applies to the current week's reading.

HOW YOU READ	WHAT YOU READ	WHAT YOU THINK
➤ I was distracted by… ➤ I started to think about… ➤ I got stuck when… ➤ I was confused/focused today because… ➤ One strategy I used to help me read this better was…. ➤ When I got distracted I tried to refocus myself by… ➤ These words or phrases were new/interesting to me…I think they mean…. ➤ When reading I should… ➤ When I read I realized that… ➤ I had a difficult time under standing… ➤ I'll read better next time if I…	➤ Why does the character/ author… ➤ Why doesn't the character/ author… ➤ What surprised me most was… ➤ I predict that… ➤ I noticed that the author uses… ➤ If I could, I'd ask the au thor… ➤ The most interesting event/ idea in this article is… ➤ I realized… ➤ The main conflict/idea in this article is… ➤ I wonder why… ➤ One theme that keeps coming up is… ➤ I found the following quote interesting…. ➤ I __________ this article because…	➤ I think _______ because… A good example of _____ is… ➤ This reminded me of _____ because… ➤ This was important because… ➤ One thing that surprised me was ______ because I always thought…. ➤ I like the way... ➤ I dislike... ➤ If I were the author, I would... ➤ My favorite part...

Search & Share

Mirroring

Vince Dang | vincedang.com

A technique called mirroring can improve your speech and your ability to monitor your pronunciation. The goal is to **study a native English speaker** on video and copy the speaker's words and gestures as you see and hear them. This will help you sound and look more like a native speaker.

1. Choose a model.
   a. This should be an American person whom you admire and want to imitate [e.g. Martin Luther King Jr., Warren Buffet, etc...].
   b. Find a video of this American native English speaker [e.g. Youtube, TEDtalk, etc...]. The speaker should be speaking for at least 3-5 minutes long.

2. Analyze the speaker and their speech.
   a. Study the video of this speaker as many times as you need to complete the assignment.
   b. Record 5 sentences that the speaker says. For each sentence, focus on 1 content word (i.e. words with meaning, such as nouns, verbs, adjectives, adverbs) to study.

3. Present your findings. You can include:
   a. Information about the speaker and how the video can be found (e.g. website address)
   b. An introduction about why you chose this speaker
   c. A conclusion about the particular way that your speaker talks. Does he use a lot of hand gestures? Does he make certain mouth movements or facial expressions when they speak? Does he pause a lot or repeat certain words frequently?

On the day of the presentation, play the video and then **mirror 1-2 minutes of the speaker you chose.** Try to copy everything the speaker says a few seconds after you hear it. Imitate the speaker's hand, face, and body movements. Notice how the movements go with the speech. You will have to practice this many times for it to get easier. The more times you repeat the mirroring, the more it will help you.

Have fun and enjoy!

Student Presentation

Reproducible

Instructor Evaluation

Speaker:____________________ Topic: ____________________

Time:____________________ Date: ____________________

Indicate the extent to which you agree with the statement on the left, using a scale of 1-4 **(1=strongly disagree; 2=disagree; 3=agree; 4=strongly agree).** Total the numbers in each column.

Evaluation Criteria	Scale	Feedback
The presenter spoke **clearly**.		
The presenter spoke at an appropriate **volume**.		
The presenter spoke at a comfortable **pace**.		
The presenter **faced** the audience.		
The presenter stood up **straight**.		
The presenter used effective hand **gestures**.		
The presenter made **eye contact**.		
The **introduction** caught my attention.		
The presenter provided some good **examples**.		
The **conclusion** wrapped up the speech.		
The speaker effectively answered questions		
Total:		

Short Answers:

What was great about this presentation?

What could have been better? What still needs to be improved?

Other observations and tips:

Two tips for the student presenter to do better on the next presentation.

1. ____
2. ____

Peer Response and a Question

Speaker: ____________________ Topic: ____________________

Time: ____________________ Date: ____________________

Short Answers:

What was great about this presentation?

What could have been better? What still needs to be improved?

Other observations and tips:

Two tips for the student presenter to do better on the next presentation.

1. ____

2. ____

"It's not that I'm so smart, it's just that I stay with problems longer."
—Albert Einstein (1879-1955), American scientist

Student Presentation

Reproducible

Name:______________________ Topic: ______________________

Time:______________________ Date: ______________________

Presentation Checklist

- o Have I practiced many times?
- o Did I get feedback from a classmate/friend?
- o Have I timed my presentation (if applicable)?
- o Do I introduce myself (if applicable)?
- o Do I maintain eye contact?
- o Do I explain my visuals (if applicable)?
- o Do I pause sometimes and check for understanding?
- o Did I look up words to correct my pronunciation?
- o Am I using appropriate volume so that everyone can hear?

Presentation Checklist

Indicate the extent to which you agree with the statement on the left, using a scale of 1-4 **(1=strongly disagree; 2=disagree; 3=agree; 4=strongly agree)**. Total the numbers in each column.

Evaluation Criteria	Scale	Feedback
I spoke clearly.		
I spoke at an appropriate volume.		
I spoke at a comfortable pace.		
I faced the audience.		
I stood up straight and looked professional.		
I used effective hand gestures.		
I made eye contact with the entire audience.		
The introduction caught the audience's attention.		
I provided some clear examples.		
I concluded the speech in an effective way		
I provided solid answers to questions		
Total:		

What do you like your presentation? What worked?

What could have done better? What still needs to be improved?

Other observations and tips:

What are two things you will do differently in your next presentation?

Survey 1

Reproducible

Interviewing International Visitors in Vietnam

Many visitors will be glad to speak with you if they know that you just want to practice your English. When finished, be sure to thank them for their time and conversation!

Speaker:________________ Location:________________

Interviewee:________________ Date:________________

Start the conversation with: "Hi! My name is.__________ Can I ask you a few questions for my English class?"

1. Where are you from? | Europe | North America | Asia | Other__________

2. What brings you to Vietnam? | Tourism | Business | Both

3. How long have you been in Vietnam? | 5 days or less | 6-13 days | 2 weeks- 2 months | Longer__________

4. What do you like about Vietnam? | Food | People | Shopping | Museums | Sights | Other

5. What else do you hope to see or do in Vietnam before you leave?

6. Will you be taking souvenirs from Vietnam back with you? What kind? Why?

7. How can you describe your visit?

8. Will you recommend a visit to Vietnam to your family and friends? Why?
   | Absolutely | Probably | Maybe | No

9. Would you please rate my English during our conversation?
   | Excellent | Very good | Good | Okay | Needs improvement

> **"You'll never know everything about anything, especially something you love."**
> —Mahatma Gandhi (1869-1948), Indian leader

Survey 2

Reproducible

Interviewing International Visitors in Vietnam

Many visitors will be glad to speak with you if they know that you just want to practice your English. When finished, be sure to thank them for their time and conversation!

Speaker: ______________________ Location: ______________________

Interviewee: ______________________ Date: ______________________

Start the conversation with:"Hi! My name is.____________Can I ask you a few questions for my English class?"

1. Where are you from? | Europe | North America | Asia | Other ____________

2. What brings you to Vietnam? | Tourism | Business | Both

3. How long have you been in Vietnam? | 5 days or less | 6-13 days | 2 weeks- 2 months | Longer ____________

4. What do you like about Vietnam? | Food | People | Shopping | Museums | Sights

____

____

5. Which Vietnamese dishes have you tried?

____

____

6. How does the food here compare with the food in your country?

____

____

7. Can you compare shopping here with your country?

____

____

8. How would you describe your visit so far?

____

____

9. Can you share three tips for other visitors coming to Vietnam?

____

____

Interviewing International Visitors in Vietnam

Many visitors will be glad to speak with you if they know that you just want to practice your English. When finished, be sure to thank them for their time and conversation!

Speaker: ______________________ Location: ______________________

Interviewee: ______________________ Date: ______________________

Start the conversation with: Hi! My name is ____________.Can I ask you a few questions for my English class?

1. Where are you from? | Europe | North America | Asia | Other ____________

2. What brings you to Vietnam? | Tourism | Business | Both

3. How long have you been in Vietnam? | 5 days or less | 6-13 days | 2 weeks- 2 months | Longer ____________

4. What do you like about Vietnam? | Food | People | Shopping | Museums | Sights | Other

____

____

5. Okay, what have you seen so far in Vietnam?

____

____

6. How do you travel from one place to another? Do you walk? Ride a motorcycle?

____

____

7. How about longer distances?

____

____

8. Where else are you going?

____

____

9. What's your best memory of Vietnam so far? Why?

____

____

APPENDIX 4

Academic Word List

The Importance of the Academic Word List

What is the Academic Word List? Why does it matter? How can it help you get a higher TOEFL Score? How can it help you learn and participate more in your college classes?

Let's start with what many Vietnamese students hoping to go to college or study abroad already know. TOEFL and IELTS scores count, and focusing on the Academic Word List (AWL) helps students score higher on the TOEFL, the IELTS, and understand more in college courses across the curriculum.

English teachers naturally notice and appreciate a strong vocabulary, and academic writing requires a more formal register than casual oral speech. Standardized tests also reward a rich vocabulary and often explicitly test vocabulary skills. Nuance and precision can also be displayed by finding the appropriate word. Therefore, English language learners naturally seek to develop a strong academic vocabulary in order to succeed as college and university students.

Yet what are the key words that a college student needs for academic success in English? Professor Averil Coxhead at the School of Linguistics and Applied Language Studies at Victoria University of Wellington, New Zealand studied a wide range of academic texts across disciplines in the late 1990s. She culled 570 word families that she deemed vital for college preparation and created the Academic Word List. The list was further divided into 10 sub-lists, from the most frequent to the least frequent.

Because of Coxhead's systematic approach and the clear need for this type of focused vocabulary list to help ambitious, college bound international students, the AWL quickly established itself within academic high schools around the world. Many intensive English programs also adopted the AWL for their college prep programs, creating a niche within the ESL/EFL world. Although an intense controversy has arisen over the extensive focus on this vocabulary list, highly motivated students (like you!) should become at least familiar with the AWL.

Let's begin with better English conversations in our English classrooms. Adding more AWL words and teaching explicit vocabulary enrichment exercises—in your writing and speaking—is a simple, effective method. Please pay extra attention to these words in your academic courses and test preparation.

"Education is the kindling of a flame, not the filling of a vessel."
—Plutarch (46 – 120), Greek biographer and historian

The following is a list of AWL words reviewed on the Vocabulary List in this textbook:

Academic	Achieve	Advocate	Assist
Accurate	Adapt	Appreciate	Assume
Available	Ethnic	Label	Recover
Bond	External	Lecture	Region
Conduct	Fee	Media	Rely
Consumer	Flexible	Medical	Resolve
Controversy	Fund	Participate	Rigid
Conversation	Generation	Positive	Role
Cooperate	Goal	Potential	Schedule
Criteria	Hierarchy	Publication	Section
Culture	Interact	Purchase	

Q Student Independent Learning for 570 AWL:
https://quizlet.com/_2lisa6

You can find the entire Academic Word List (AWL) in 10 subsections online:

https://simple.wiktionary.org/wiki/Wiktionary:Academic_word_list

Source: Wikitionary – Academic Word List accessed on 7/30/16.

We also strongly recommend English language learners become familiar with the Corpus of Contemporary American English (COCA). This amazing reference site documents how English words and phrases actually appear in spoken and written English. Checking the use of AWL words, especially when combined with prepositions and in collocations, will help English students improve the accuracy and fluency. You can become a savvy word detective by regularly consulting COCA. Does that sound like a plan?

Source: http://corpus.byu.edu/coca/

"One forgets words as one forgets names.
One's vocabulary needs constant fertilizing or it will die."
—Evelyn Waugh (1903-1966), British author and journalist

APPENDIX 5

Prefixes and Suffixes

Most Common Prefixes

Prefix	Meaning	between
anti-	against	middle
de-	down	wrongly
dis-	not, opposite, away	not
en- **em-**	put into, cover with	enclose embrace
fore-	before	forecast
in-	in	insert
in- **im** **il-** **ir-**	not	incomplete impatient illegal irregular
inter-	between	intersect
mid-	middle	midterm
mis-	wrongly	misplace
non-	not	nonfiction
over-	over	overlook
pre-	before	precook
re-	again	reappear
semi-	half	semicircle
sub-	under	subway
super-	above	superman
trans-	across	transfer
un-	not	uncommon
under-	under	underwater

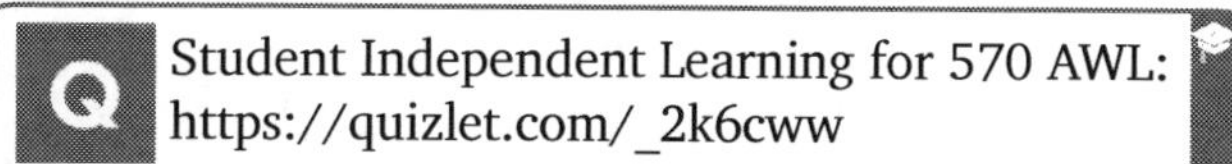

Most Common Suffixes

Suffix	Meaning	between
able -ible	can be done	agreeable edible
-al	act/process of	refusal
-ed	past-tense verbs	smiled
-en	made of	brighten
-er	comparative (2 items)	taller
-er	person who	dancer
-est	superlative (2+ items)	largest
-ful	full of	cheerful
-ic -ical	having characteristics of	domestic musical
-ing	action/gerund	shopping
-ion -tion -ation	act, process	occasion transition complication
-ity -ty	state of	serenity
-ize	to become	socialize
-less	without, not affected by	tireless
-ly	characteristic of	quickly
-ment	action/process of	enjoyment
-ness	state of, condition of	wilderness
-ous -ious	having the qualities of	joyous studious
-s -es	plural	schools boxes
-y	full of	messy

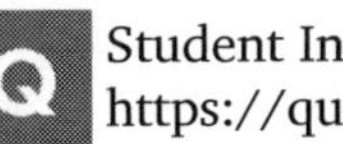

Student Independent Learning for 570 AWL:
https://quizlet.com/_2k6983

"It is a familiar and significant saying that a problem well put is half-solved."
—John Dewey (1859-1952), American educator

Recommended Supplemental Websites

Online English as a Foreign Language (EFL) Resources to Keep Learning English

Accurate English
Lisa Mojsin works on helping students improve their English through accent reduction courses.
www.accurateenglish.com

Compelling Conversations
Visit our website to keep in touch, download free ESL/EFL work-sheets, and learn about more books for English Language learners.
www.CompellingConversations.com

English Daily
Links for ESL students like downloading English books, learning American Slang expressions, and English grammar.
Fun activities like chatting and some activities to how to learn English.
http://www.englishdaily626.com/

ESL-lab
A deep, excellent resource for adult ESL students with developed listening exercises for low, intermediate, and high-intermediate students. Practical and impressive!
www.esl-lab.com

Free Rice
As students build their vocabulary repertoire, they are also helping end world hunger.
http://www.freerice.com

Guide to English Grammar and Writing
A valuable online collection of free tools, quizzes, and worksheets to help Capital Community college students improve their grammar and writing skills.
www.grammar.ccc.commnet.edu/grammar

Internet TESL Journal's Self-Study Quizzes for ESL Students
Self-study quizzes for ESL students including grammar and vocabulary quizzes.
Free games, quizzes and puzzles that you can play online.
http://a4esl.org/q/h/

Learner's Dictionary
A free online dictionary designed to help ESL students understand new vocabulary words because of its simplistic definitions and example sentences.
http://www.learnersdictionary.com/

Many Things
A rich resource for English language learners at multiple levels. The site includes vocabulary quizzes, proverb quizzes, and idioms games.
www.manythings.org

Online Writing Lab (OWL)
Writing tips from Purdue University's acclaimed Online Writing Lab (OWL). Includes excellent ESL tips.
www.owl.english.purdue.edu/owl

Randall's ESL Cyber Listening Lab
Free audio and video quizzes (including related software) for all levels of English learners and links to other listening sites.
http://www.esl-lab.com/

TED Talks
Hear some of the world's leading experts speak about a wide variety of topics. Most talks are 15–20 minutes long, but you can start with the short talks of less than six minutes. Many videos include subtitles too.
www.Ted.com

The Internet TESL Journal
Useful links such as tests, quizzes, listening, vocabulary, spelling, speaking, reading, and more.
http://iteslj.org/links/ESL/

This I Believe
This nonprofit educational website includes thousands of essays and podcasts about personal beliefs. It is widely used by American high school and college English departments to both encourage and showcase personal essays.
www.thisibelieve.com

USA Learns
This U.S. Department of Education website combines video lessons and clear written English for new English language learners worldwide.
www.usalearns.org

Using English
Resources for learning the English language for ESL, EFL, ESOL, and EAP students and teachers. It has online tests and quizzes that are useful for ESL students.
http://www.usingenglish.com/

Voice of America
This wonderful public radio website is designed for English language learners. Short, slow radio reports look at American history, national parks, the English language, and current news.
www.voanews.com/learningenglish

"All the world is my school and all humanity is my teacher."
—George Whitman(1913-2011), Founder of Shakespeare and Company

Recommended Supplemental Apps

EasyBib is a tool that helps you create citations in MLA, APA and Chicago/Turabian styles. With EasyBib you can create a works cited list and parenthetical (in-text) citations. Great for research or advance writing classes!

GammarUp have different sections of the app devoted to different parts of speech (e.g. adjectives, adverbs, causative verbs, and conditionals). Each section has the technical definition of the part of speech followed by a test for students to take and practice.

Words with Friends is a multi-player word game in which players take turns building words crossword puzzle style in a manner similar to the classic board game Scrabble. It helps develop spelling and build vocabulary by encouraging word formation.

Speak English allows you to listen to recordings of English speakers talking about a span of topics – like job interviews or customer service. After listening to it as many times as you'd like, then you can then re-cord yourself repeating the phrase.

FluentU offers language immersion through native videos. Their method allows you to learn words in context in a natural way because it takes real-world videos—like music videos, commercials, news, cartoons and inspiring talks—and turns them into English learning experiences.

Business Insider is an American business, celebrity, and technology news app that will keep students on the latest news so that they can easily have small talks with native English speakers.

TOEFL Go! is the only official TOEFL® app from ETS, the maker of the TOEFL® test.

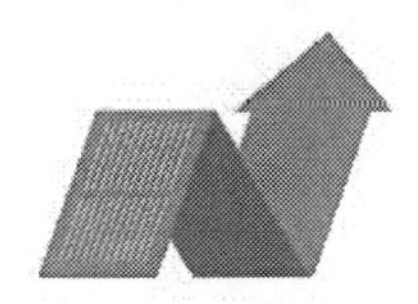

Newsmart takes daily contents from Wall Street Journal's articles and turns them into English lessons for English and Business English students. Each article is labeled by Learning Level so students can read at their own level.

Bibliography

21st Century Dictionary of Quotations. Dell Publishing, 1993. Ackerman, Mary Alice. *Conversations on the Go*. Search Institute, 2004.

Akbar, Fatollah. *The Eye of an Ant: Persian Proverbs and Poems*. Iranbooks, 1995.

Asitimbay, Diane. *What's Up, America? Second Edition. A Foreigner's Guide to Understanding Americans*. Culturelink Press, 2009.

Ben Shea, Noah. *Great Jewish Quotes: Five Thousand Years of Truth and Humor from the Bible to George Burns*. Ballantine Books, 1993.

Berman, Louis A. *Proverb Wit and Wisdom: A Treasury of Proverbs, Parodies, Quips, Quotes, Cliches, Catchwords, Epigrams, and Aphorisms*. Perigee Book,1997.

Burns, Walton. *50 Activities for the First Day of School (Teacher Tools)*. Alphabet Publishing. 2016.

Byrne, Robert. *1,911 Best Things Anybody Ever Said*. Ballantine Books, 1988.

Folse, Keith. *The Art of Teaching Speaking: Research and Pedagogy for the ESL/EFL Classroom*. Univeristy of Michigan Press ELT, 4th Edition. 2006.

Galef, David. *Even Monkeys Fall From Trees: The Wit and Wisdom of Japanese Proverbs*. Tuttle Publishing, 1987.

Galef, David. *Even a Stone Buddha Can Talk: More Wit and Wisdom of Japanese Proverbs*. Tuttle Publishing, 2000.

Gross, John. *The Oxford Book of Aphorisms*. Oxford University Press, 1987.

Habibian, Simin K. *1001 Persian-English Proverbs: Learning Language and Culture Through Commonly Used Sayings*. Third Edition. Ibex Publishers, 2002.

Houston, Hall. *Provoking Thought: Memory and Thinking in ELT*. Booksurge. 2009.

Lewis, Edward and Myers, Robert. *A Treasury of Mark Twain: The Greatest Humor of the Greatest American Humorist*. Hallmark Cards, 1967.

McWilliams, Peter. *Life 101: Everything We Wish We Had Learned About Life In School—But Didn't.*Prelude Press, 1991.

Marianne Celce-Murcia, Donna Brinton, Marguerite Ann Snow, and David Bohike. *Teaching English as a Second or Foreign Languge, 4th Edition.* Heinle ELT. 2013.

The Oxford Dictionary of Quotations, 5th Edition. Oxford University Press, 1999.

Peter, Dr. Laurence J. *Peter's Quotations: Ideas for Our Time*. William Morrow,1977.

Planaria J. Price and Euphronia Awakuni. *Life in the USA: An Immigrant's Guide to Understanding Americans*. University of Michigan Press ELT. 2009.

Quotable Quotes: Wit and Wisdom for All Occasions From America's Most Popular Magazine. Reader's Digest, 1997.

Rosten, Leo. *Rome Wasn't Burned in a Day; The Mischief of Language.* Doubleday, 1972.

Rosten, Leo. *Leo Rosten's Carnival of Wit.* Penguin Books USA, 1994.

Williams, Rose. *Latin Quips at Your Fingertips: Witty Latin Sayings by Wise Romans.* Barnes and Noble, 2000.

Winokur, Jon. **The Portable Curmudgeon.** New American Library, 1987.

Winkour, Jon. *The Traveling Curmudgeon.* Sasquatch Books, 2003.

Yong-chol, Kim. *Proverbs East and West: An Anthology of Chinese, Korean, and Japanese Saying with Western Equivalents.* Hollym, 1991.

The internet has dramatically expanded our access to quotations. A few other websites deserve to be mentioned as outstanding sources:

- http://en.wikiquote.org
- www.bartleby.com/quotations
- www.qotd.org
- www.quotationspage.com
- www.thinkexist.com

Other reference websites:

- http://corpus.byu.edu/coca/
- http://nobelprize.org
- http://www.dumblaws.com

"Some books are to be tasted, other to be swallowed, and a few to be chewed and digested."
—Sir Francis Bacon(1561-1626), English scientist

About the Authors

Teresa X. Nguyen,
M.A. in Linguistics, B.A. in English Literature, brings considerable experience to this innovative textbook for Vietnamese learners seeking to improve their English speaking skills. Currently a core faculty at the California State University, Fullerton (CSUF) in the American Language Program (ALP), she has spent over ten years directing and teaching English to Vietnamese learners, both abroad in Southeast Asia and locally in southern California.

Nguyen's thirst to sharpen her teaching skills, has led her to seize many opportunities to teach a wide variety of English language learners. Nguyen has taught English language learners in China, Vietnam, and the United States from over 25 countries. She has also taught English learners from elementary school to graduate students. The experiential basis for this communicative ESL textbook is her own struggles and successes as an international student studying abroad in Korea (2006), Spain (2007), and China (2008).

Nguyen has also presented at several English teacher conferences, including TESOL international conferences in Baltimore, Maryland (2016) & Toronto, Canada (2015), CATESOL conferences in Anaheim, California (2015) & Santa Clara, California (2014), and at TESOL club events (2014, 2015). Her presentations focus on the optimal use of edtech and accessible pedagogy. However, Nguyen's most rewarding career experience – so far – has been supervising and training TESOL graduate students as a Master teacher (2013-present).

Compelling Conversations – Vietnam: Speaking Exercises for Vietnamese Learners of English is her first book. Today, as a more successful language learning adult, she hopes to share these effective strategies through this innovative speaking skills textbook.

 **https://www.linkedin.com/in/teresaxn**

Eric H. Roth
teaches international graduate students the pleasures and perils of academic writing and public speaking in English at the University of Southern California (USC) as a Master Lecturer. He also consults with English language schools on communicative methods to effectively teach English.

Given a full scholarship as a Lilly Scholar, Roth studied philosophy and American history at Wabash College (1980-1984), and received his M.A. in Media Studies from the New School (1988). Since 1992, Roth has taught English to high school, community college, adult, and university students.

Highlights include teaching USC writing courses in Spain (2007) and Paris, France (2008); and directing the APU International High School in Ho Chi Minh City, Vietnam (2009). USC also awarded Roth two USC Teaching with Technology grants in 2012. He has also given several TESOL presentations since 2011, and has helped USC students applying for Fulbright positions as English Teaching Assistants (ETA) since 2012.

Roth co-authored Compelling Conversations: Questions and Quotations on Timeless Topics in 2006 to help English language learners increase their English fluency. Recommended by *English Teaching Professional* magazine, this advanced ESL textbook has been used in over 50 countries in English classrooms and conversation clubs. *Easy English Times*, an adult literacy newspaper, has published a monthly column, "Instant Conversation Activities," based on the book since 2008. The first specific version for a particular country, Vietnam, was published in 2011. Compelling American Conversations: Questions and Quotations for Intermediate American English Language Learners appeared in 2012 and a Teacher Edition followed in 2015. Compelling Conversations – Japan came out in 2015. Future versions for Brazil, South Korea, and Israel, are anticipated.

A member of the USC faculty since 2003, Roth is also a member of numerous professional organizations including: California Association of Teaching English to Speakers of Other Languages (CATESOL); the International Communication Association (ICA); the International Professors Project (IPP); and Teaching English to Speakers of Other Languages (TESOL). Roth has given several CATESOL conference presentations and led many teacher training worshops. Roth first visited Vietnam in 2000, and has returned three times to consult and teach. He also serves on the Fulbright National Screening Committee for English Teaching Assistants for Southeast Asia (Vietnam). He looks forward to learning more about Vietnam and engaging in many compelling conversations with Vietnamese English language learners and other English speakers in the future.

https://www.linkedin.com/in/erichroth

Toni Aberson

(M.A. English; M.A. Psychology and Religion) brings 35 years of teaching English and supervising English teachers to her materials writing. "The challenge for English teachers is to put our students at ease and encourage them to practice English," notes Aberson. "What better way than to ask students about their lives?"

Aberson also co-wrote Compelling Conversations: Questions and Quotations on Timeless Topics (2007), and Compelling American Conversations: Questions and Quotations for Intermediate American English Language English Language Learners (2012). She also wrote It's a Breeze: 42 Lively ESL Lessons on American Idioms (2012) which focuses on common expressions used in everyday situations. This is the second Compelling Conversations book that she has edited for Chimayo Press.

"I love teaching English," Aberson says. "The key in a classroom is engagement and people become interested and excited when they're learning about the daily stuff of life. When they are thinking and writing and talking about their real lives—food, jobs, family, homes, sports, movies—that's when they learn the language. Learning English is not easy. It can be a real challenge, but it can also be fun and stimulating. That's what I'm aiming for—the real life and the fun that stimulates immigrants and English students so they want to learn more. They want to jump in."

Acknowledgements

Being raised as a 1.5 generation, with dual identities as an American and as a Vietnamese, I wanted my first creative piece to accurately reflect this blessing. As a result, I wanted to collaborate with Eric on this speaking skills book for Vietnamese learners of English.

Although this text speaks with the voices of its two authors, it symbolizes the contributions of many generous individuals I'm proud to call friends and supporters. We appreciatively acknowledge these contributions and thank these individuals, whose special expertise made this second edition of Compelling Conversations: Vietnam even better and stronger.

We are indebted to the following photographers for their astonishing pictures:

- Tung Phan, Ho Chi Minh City, Vietnam
- Duong Trinh, Ha Noi, Vietnam
- Billy Pham, Oklahoma City, U.S.A.
- Tyler Tai Nguyen, Atlanta, U.S.A.
- Donovan Bui, Orange County, U.S.A.
- Vince Dang, Orange County, U.S.A.
- Clara Hutzler, Orange County, U.S.A.
- Jason Q. Tran, Orange County, U.S.A.
- Mindy Bao Ngoc, Orange County, U.S.A.
- Kim Ngo, Orange County, U.S.A.

We are indebted to the following reviewers for their constructive feedback:

Annie Tran, Orange County, U.S.A.
Tremonisha Putros, Orange County, U.S.A.
Kim Nguyen, Ho Chi Minh City, Vietnam

We are indebted to Keyon Nguyen for the wonderful layout vision of this text.

And last but definitely not least, I'm indebted to Eric Roth for his willingness to collaborate with me to make this dream a reality.

Thank you again friends and supporters for helping make my first book a satisfying creative success.

Teresa X. Nguyen
Co-Author, Compelling Conversations: Vietnam

"Gratitude is the memory of the heart."
—French proverb

Step by step, we move forward. Several educators, friends, and colleagues have helped in the creation of this dramatically revised English conversation textbook for Vietnamese students. Numerous English language professionals and students have made sensible suggestions at critical moments. Allow me to publicly thank a few by name.

I remain especially grateful to seven individuals: Teresa X. Nguyen, Andrea Schmidt, Dr. Binh Tran, Mai-Anh Nwin, Steve Riggs, Toni Aberson, and Laurie Selik. Teresa, a dedicated and energetic professor at California State University - Fullerton in the American Language Program, envisioned an expanded, improved, and visually more attractive second edition of Compelling Conversations -Vietnam. This summer we started working together. It's been a distinct pleasure to share ideas and craft new materials for Vietnamese learners of English in the United States and elsewhere. Andrea helped edit and design this new edition. Thank you!

This new edition of Compelling Conversations: Vietnam builds on the original book released five years ago. Dr. Binh and Mai-Anh from APU International High School originally suggested transforming an ESL book for American immigrants into a specialized EFL textbook so many moons ago. Steve, Toni, and Laurie helped edit the original EFL speaking skills book, asked many questions and made the book work better for English learners. This version builds on their many contributions and insights. Thank you!

Several other Vietnamese educators, EFL professionals, fellow English teachers, and Vietnamese-American colleagues and friends also made helpful suggestions. While we can't list everyone by name, it's a pleasure to acknowledge the efforts of so many fine folks. A friendly spirit of collaboration and conversation created this second edition.

Finally, I would like to thank the dedicated English students who worked with us during the last decade. From Ho Chi Minh City to the University of Southern California to UC Riverside and Santa Monica Community College, you have shared your insights and created compelling classroom conversations. Your progress inspires. .

Naturally, we take full responsibility for any mistakes, omissions, or imperfections.
May we all keep learning and sharing as our world continues to rapidly change in the 21st century. Let us always strive to become better communicators and better people.

Eric H. Roth
Co-Author, Compelling Conversations: Vietnam

Critical Praise for the Compelling Conversations Series

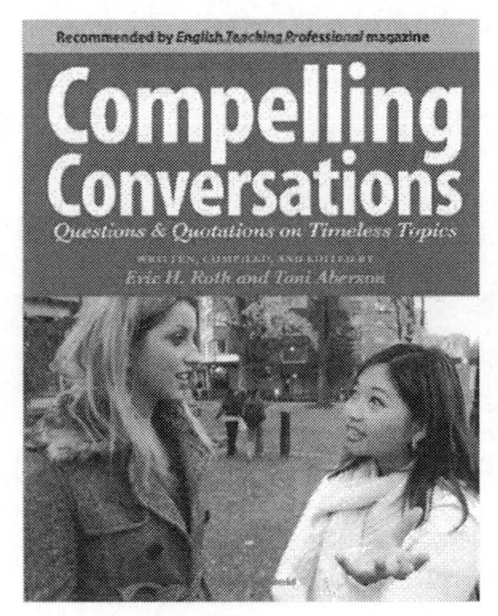

Compelling Conversations

"In my own teaching, I have found questions and quotations to be highly effective in promoting student discussion. Questions are useful in that they require a response from the listener. Asking them also helps students master the tricky rules of the interrogative. Quotations are brilliant flashes of wit expressed in the shortest space possible, often just a sentence or two. The authors have compiled a formidable collection of quotations by famous people. The authors also add some wise proverbs here and there. My two favorites were 'Recite patience three times and it will spare you a murder' and 'When money talks, truth keeps silent,' which are from Korea and Russia. In sum, Compelling Conversations is a recommended resource for teachers who want to make their conversation classes more learner-centered. It should be especially appealing to those who wish to escape the confines of the Presentation -Practice-Production approach and do without a formal grammatical or functional syllabus. It reflects the authors' considerable professional experience, and would be a notable addition to any English teacher's bookshelf."

—Hall Houston English Teaching Professional magazine (January 2009)

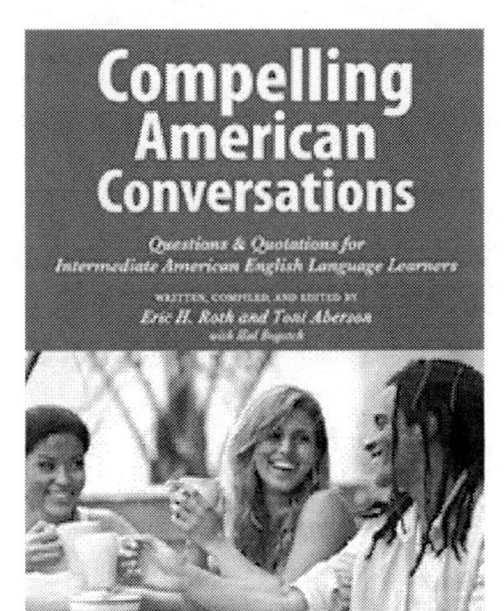

Compelling American Conversations

"How can so much learning be in just one book? Compelling American Conversations is all that an ESL teacher or student needs to use in their course. With clear, easy-to-follow directions, students learn necessary details about American English and culture, practice critical thinking, and expand vocabulary and idioms as they converse in real, natural adult English. Included in the "Search and Share" component are marvelous lessons on using the Internet. An extra bonus is that any of the conversations, quotes, etc. can be used as writing prompts. The book is fun and stimulating and, fortunately, very accessible for the intermediate learner."

—Planaria Price Author, Life in the USA and Realistically Speaking

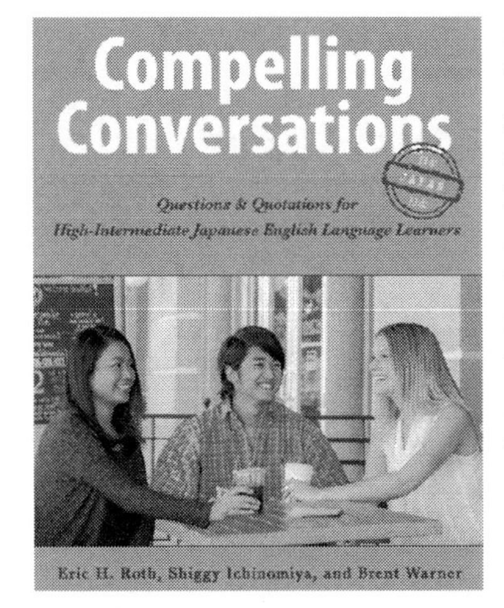

Compelling Conversations - Japan

"As an ESL teacher and accent reduction coach, I regularly encounter frustrated students from Japan who don't feel comfortable speaking English. Compelling Conversations – Japan will prove very useful to Japanese English Language Learners ... It's more than just a conversation book; it's also a cross-cultural awareness book, filled with proverbs and cultural insights. In addition, it features valuable English pronunciation exercises focusing on the sounds that are difficult for native Japanese speakers. It also contains numerous fun and thought-provoking conversation topics relevant to a person from a Japanese cultural background."

—Lisa Mojsin, Author, Mastering the American Accent

About Chimayo Press

Sophisticated English for Global Souls

CHIMAYO PRESS is an independent educational publishing company committed to publishing niche books that create compelling conversations, deepen relationships, and celebrate the human spirit. We launched in 2005 with one advanced level English as a Second Language (ESL) title—Compelling Conversations: Questions and Quotations on Timeless Topics—from authors Eric H. Roth and Toni Aberson. This fluency-focused English textbook has blossomed into a series that meets the varying needs of English language learners and teachers in over 50 countries.

Compelling Conversations has also become the foundation for an expanding number of ESL and EFL (English as a Foreign Language) titles. The Compelling Conversations: Questions and Quotations series includes national versions for Vietnamese learners of American English (2011), American immigrants and refugees (2012), Japanese English language learners (2015). In 2012, we also published It's a Breeze: 42 Lively Lessons on American Idioms. This book, Compelling Conversations – Vietnam: Speaking Exercises for Vietnamese Learners of English (Teresa X. Nguyen and Roth) takes the series to a new level.

Janet Levine and Laurie Selik expanded the series to include professional books for native English speakers. Compelling Conversations for Fundraisers: Talk Your Way to Success with Donors and Funders (2016) continues the focus on building stronger relationships through better conversations. Future titles will include Compelling Conversations for Call Center Professionals and Compelling Conversations for Global Business Professionals.

As a small publisher, we are grateful for each purchase of our books. We have a growing list of both nonfiction and fiction titles—our authors include working English teachers, radio professionals, and screenwriters. Each distinctive book reflects the passion and perspectives of the authors. Visit www.ChimayoPress.com to see our growing catalog. English language teachers, tutors, and students are also invited to visit www.compellingconversations.com for more conversation materials and teacher tips.

Chimayo Press is named for our amazingly communicative, talented, and loving first border collie. We met Chimayo soon after a visit to the inspirational New Mexico town on a cross-country trip from Chicago to Los Angeles back in the 20th century. That's Chimayo's image in our logo.

Would you like to review this book? We'd love to receive your feedback, read a positive review on Amazon, and start another new conversation!

Ask more. Know more. Share more.
Create Compelling Conversations.
www.CompellingConversations.com

Made in the USA
San Bernardino, CA
25 March 2017